Best
Tea Shop Walks
in
KENT

Norman & June Buckley

Published by Sigma Leisure – an imprint of
Sigma Press, 1 South Oak Lane, Wilmslow, Cheshire SK9 6AR, England.

British Library Cataloguing in Publication Data
A CIP record for this book is available from the British Library.

ISBN: 1-85058-734-5

Typesetting and Design by: Sigma Press, Wilmslow, Cheshire.

Cover photographs: main photograph, The Copper Kettle at Chilham; smaller photographs, from top, Chatwell; Brogden fruit farm; Sandwich *(all cover photographs, copyright June Buckley)*

Maps: Jeremy Semmens

Photographs: Norman Buckley

Printed by: MFP Design and Print

Disclaimer: the information in this book is given in good faith and is believed to be correct at the time of publication. No responsibility is accepted by either the author or publisher for errors or omissions, or for any loss or injury howsoever caused. Only you can judge your own fitness, competence and experience.

Contents

The Walks

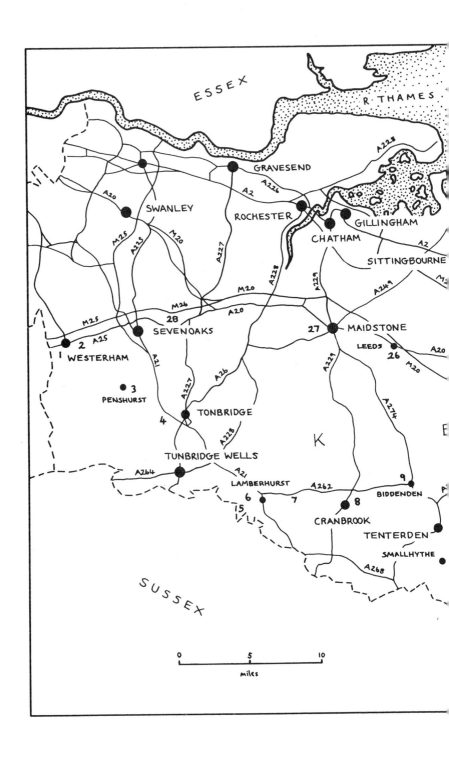

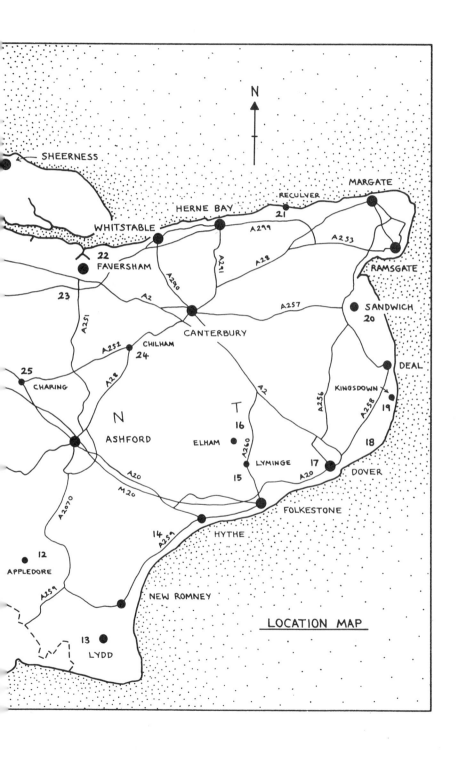

LOCATION MAP

Introduction

Landscape

The great West to East sweep of the North Downs separates the bulk of Kent from the Thames Basin and its huge London conurbation. The ridge of the Downs then bears a little to the south to head for the Dover/Folkestone area where its outcropping at the English Channel provides Kent with much the finest part of its coastline. This chalk land of the Downs is the small residue of a huge dome which once overlaid the whole of south east England. Closely adjacent to the south side of the chalk is a ridge of Greensand, a comparatively impermeable clay, then comes the Weald, a large, ill-defined, area including part of East Sussex, in which the rich agricultural potential has long justified the 'Garden of England' label, nestling within the protective arm thrown round it by the Downs.

It would be over simplistic and incorrect to see this countryside in terms of Downs – high and sparse, Weald – low and richly fertile, as is the case, for example, in much of Wiltshire. The Kent Downs are not really high – 245m (804 ft) at best, and the Weald is, in part, sufficiently undulating to justify the use of the term 'High Weald', particularly appropriate in the Goudstone area. Consequently, very little of the Downland is really wild and the demarcation between the two areas is seldom abrupt. Between the Downs and the North Sea are more areas of predominantly low-lying land, largely characterised by the series of 'islands', some of which have long been firmly attached to the 'mainland'.

The Kentish Weald has long been famous for orchards and hops which, combined with features such as the former oast houses and weatherboarded buildings, produce a highly characteristic landscape. Despite the difficulties arising from supermarket type trading and a great increase in apple imports, many orchards are still alive and well. Likewise, the consumer shift away from traditional draft beers to lager, mostly imported, has reduced but not eliminated the demand for hop production.

It is fair to say that, outside the major towns, today's landscape is little affected by traditional industry, other than that associated with the construction of roads and the major new continental rail link. Evidence on the ground that parts of the Weald were the cradle of the British iron industry is scant indeed although the activity was on a scale sufficient to consume a sizeable forest. Proximity to London and the consequent pressure for development land means that abandoned industrial sites have not been left derelict or preserved as museums, as might well have been the case in a more remote, poorer, area. A more recent example is the Kent coal industry, where the mines working the coal field situated between Canterbury and Dover were abruptly closed down some years after World War II and have seemingly been air-brushed from the scene; it does not even merit a mention in material prepared for visitors by the tourism industry.

Kent has only one important river, the Medway, which links large towns such as Tonbridge and Maidstone with the historic ports and former naval area of Rochester, Chatham and Gillingham, close to the estuary. The much less important Great Stour rises to the north west of Ashford, passes through that town, then cuts through the Downs between Wye and Chilham. After passing through Canterbury, it meanders towards Thanet before reaching the sea at Sandwich. Overall it does seem that rivers play a relatively minor part in the appreciation of the Kent landscape.

Early occupation

Of the Early Stone Age, only a few rock shelters at Oldbury Hill provide any evidence of the presence of the hunter/gatherer people who roamed over what is now Kent. Several long barrows and similar burial chambers mark the presence of Neolithic occupants. Three are in the Wrotham area; the two Kits Coty chambers, plus a jumbled heap of Sarsen stones are a few miles south of Rochester; Julliberrie's Grave is close to Chilham. The Bronze Age has left very little, just the Ringwould round barrows, 4 miles north of Dover. The Iron Age was the time of the construction of earth banked forts, very often on hill tops, in most parts of the country. The four known sites in Kent are at Tunbridge Wells High Rocks, Squerryes Park, Bigbury and Oldbury. The small, nucleated settlements which housed the Bronze Age farmers and their families, surrounded by the small 'Celtic' fields which provided their livelihood, set the pattern for much of the landscape, changing gently over the centuries until the mechanisation of the later 20th century finally swept away so many of the remaining ancient hedgerow boundaries and so many old villages had extensive residential estates grafted on.

The 'Gateway to England'

As the part of Britain closest to continental Europe, it was inevitable that from earliest times raiders and invaders would be most likely to land on these largely unprotected shores. For some decades from about 120BC, waves of immigrants from what is now the area of Belgium (the Belgae) landed in Kent and by the mouth of the Thames. In 55BC and again in 54BC Julius Caesar landed in Kent on his exploratory expeditions, conquering much of the south east, then occupied by the Cantiaci Belgic tribe. Caesar pushed as far north as Hertfordshire, subduing the Catuvellauni, before returning to Rome. Friendly enough relations lasted for nearly 100 years, as long as the English tribes remained subservient to Rome, paying annual tribute money. However, towards the end of this period relations were disrupted, largely by the belligerence of the Catuvellauni. The full scale invasion followed in AD43, when Roman forces landed at Richborough, which soon became established as a fort and as the principal entrance port to Britain. As the Roman occupation and influence faded in the 5th century AD, so Saxon invaders arrived and settled in Kent in considerable numbers; their best known leaders were Hengist and Horsa. In AD597 a peaceful invasion with far reaching implications took place at Pegwell Bay, near Ramsgate, when St. Augustine landed with a few followers. He continued through Kent and beyond to convert Britain to Christianity, founding Canterbury Cathedral. During their prolonged period of raiding and eventually settling in Britain, the Vikings included Kent among the many places at which they landed. The great Norman invasion of 1066 missed landing in Kent by only a few miles, but later French invaders came and went with the ebb and flow of conflict during the period when some Kings of England lived for long periods in France, besieging Dover Castle and burning churches in the south of the county. During the reign of King Henry VIII, constant fears of invasion by the French and Spanish prompted the building of coastal defensive castles such as Deal and Walmer. The threatened attack was long delayed and everyone knows that the great Armada was dispersed and largely destroyed before a landing could be made in Kent or any other part of the south coast.

There were, in fact, no further invasions through this gateway to Britain, but threats, such as those by Napoleon in the early 19th century, were sufficient to provoke defensive provisions such as the construction of the numerous Martello Towers and the Royal Military Canal. Likewise, in recent times, Hitler's stated intentions resulted in improvements to the coastal defences and the provision of 'front line' fighter airfields such as the famous Biggin Hill.

Castles and Stately Homes

As would be expected in a vulnerable 'gateway' area, many defensive castles were built in Kent. Some, such as Leeds and Hever, have subsequently been modified to provide stately homes, whilst others, such as Tonbridge and Deal, lie in ruins. One of our greatest of all castles, at Dover, survives as a wonderful attraction for visitors. Great stately homes include Knole, claimed to be the largest in England, and Penshurst.

Most of the castles and stately homes are surrounded by great swathes of parkland and, very often, substantial ornamental gardens. Either the National Trust or English Heritage are heavily involved in the restoration and maintenance of a good number of these properties.

Churches and Cathedrals

Kent claims to be the only county with two cathedrals. Everyone knows about Canterbury, a magnificent medieval structure on a site made holy by St. Augustine at the very dawn of Anglo-Saxon Christianity, seat of the Archbishop of Canterbury, head of the Anglican Church and for centuries a destination for pilgrims, with well-trod routes from London and from Winchester. Thanks to Chaucer's 'Canterbury Tales, we know more about medieval pilgrimages to Canterbury than to any other site in the world. Less well known is the cathedral at Rochester, in the Medway valley, an impressive place, with the oldest cathedral nave in England.

As in so many counties of England, for eight hundred years or more the churches of Kent have provided an enduring backbone to the county's history. Nowhere is there a richer heritage of Saxon construction retained and sometimes reworked into a later, Norman, structure. The size and splendour of some of these churches has resulted in the 'Cathedral of ...' title being unofficially applied in several cases. Although less pronounced than in, say, the Cotswolds or Suffolk, the wealth generated by the wool trade has played a part in funding some of the grandest of these churches. The historic interest of the structures is frequently matched by the wealth and variety of internal furnishings; brasses and other monuments to generations of noble families are particularly prolific in the county.

The Coast

Apart from the defensive considerations mentioned above, proximity to London has ensured that the era of the seaside holiday which commenced with the building of the railways in the mid 19th century, had a great effect on the landscape of the Kent coast. Several areas, particularly the Isle of Thanet, saw the rapid development of what had been villages into populous resorts such as Whitstable, Margate, Herne Bay and Ramsgate, eventually coalescing into a continuous strip catering for mass holiday requirements, both for those who could afford to stay for a week or more and those who, because of the comparatively short, quick, journey, could make the 'day trip'. The rise of the cheap foreign package holiday in the past 40 years has had the obvious effect on this area; the resorts are having to come to terms with tourism on a much reduced scale. Hythe and Deal are other, rather low key, resorts, in each case firmly based on nice old towns. Hythe is further from London and has probably been less subject to the fluctuations, up and down, of the Thanet coast. The ports of Dover and Folkestone, with cross channel travel at a high level despite the tunnel and cheap air fares, still have an important role in facilitating the 'Gateway to England' role of Kent. Despite some extravagant claims, much of the undeveloped part of the Kent coastline is flat and marshy, of little interest to the visitor apart from dedicated bird watchers. The white cliffs of the Dover area, extending for several miles are, of course, magnificent and have acquired a unique symbolism over the centuries.

The Future

The future depends largely on the answers to two important questions. Reverting to the opening of this introduction; how much more work will need be carried out on major road and rail projects, carving out great swathes of this vulnerable countryside to carry millions of people ever more quickly, primarily between London and the coast? The second question is: will our town and country planners and their political masters be willing and able to resist the great pressures, financial and otherwise, which will increasingly attempt to push development out from London across the North

Downs and to expand from existing towns and villages further to the centre and south of the county, irrespective of green belts, Areas of Outstanding Natural Beauty and other restraints?

The future of Kent as a rural county, attractive to walkers and other country lovers depends heavily on the outcome of these issues.

1. Westerham and Chartwell

A delightful walk, largely in woodland, linking the pleasant small town of Westerham with one of Britain's most cherished National Trust properties, the former family home of Sir Winston Churchill. The length of the walk is modest, but there is a fair amount of up and down, including two short, steep, sections. Underfoot, the various tracks and footpaths, including a length of the Greensand Way, are very good, with less than half a km (a third of a mile) along the side of a minor road. Eight stiles.

Distance: 7.5km (4¾ miles).

Start/car parking: A small free car park in the middle of Westerham — from the High Street turn north along London Road for 100 metres; the car park is on the left, grid reference 446540. Otherwise find any town centre car park There is a large edge of town car park near Quebec House on the eastern fringe.

Maps: Ordnance Survey Explorer 147, Sevenoaks and Tonbridge, 1:25,000. Ordnance Survey Landranger 187, Dorking, Reigate and Crawley (part), Ordnance Survey Landranger 188, Maidstone and the Weald (part), 1:50,000.

Tea Shop

This lovely walk offers a choice of café. Perhaps ramblers may even like to consider lunch at one and indulge in tea at the other. Fortunately the walk, especially if visits to Chartwell House and gardens are included, uses quite a lot of energy to burn-off the extra calorific intake. The café at Chartwell can be accessed even if not visiting the National Trust property. Between 12 noon and 2pm, soup and rolls and hot dishes such as salmon fillet with strawberry and wine sauce, or salads, are available; and delicious puddings too! There is a special menu for children. From the afternoon selection are delicacies such as orange spice cake and the Chartwell cream tea. Fresh strawberries served with cream are served subject to availability. As well as the large tea room there is a sunny terrace and a roofed veranda.

Open: 1ˢᵗ April (or Easter) to the end of October, Wednesday to Sunday and Bank Holiday Monday 10.30am to 5pm. Also open on

Tuesdays in July and August. During November and December open 11am – 4pm. Tel. 01732 863087.

The other venue is in Westerham. 'Tiffins' faces The Green and is a luxurious teashop with basket chairs and bone china. The menu lists sandwiches such as ham or egg and cress served on white or granary bread. There is a good selection of cakes; buttered tea bread is also available. Leaf tea is served here – welcome and quite unusual these days – with strainer provided. Filtered coffee and hot chocolate with cream are also available.

Open: Wednesday to Saturday, 11am to 4.30pm. Sunday, 12.30 to 5pm. Closed on Monday & Tuesday. Hours could vary so if in any doubt do telephone first. Tel. 01959 562564.

Introduction

Despite having the A25 main road as its High Street, Westerham is a charming little town with an old market place and a triangular green surrounded by houses of the 17th and 18th centuries. On the green stand statues of two of the most famous men associated with the town. Firstly, James Wolfe who, as a very young general, led the British forces in the spectacular storming of the Heights of Abraham near Quebec in the war against the French in Canada, perishing in the conflict, was brought up in Westerham. Secondly, and of more recent memory, is Sir Winston Churchill, who made nearby Chartwell his home from the 1920s. This statue is by Oscar Neman. On the eastern edge of Westerham, Wolfe's former home, the lovely 17th-century, red-brick Quebec House, is now in the ownership of the National Trust and is open to the public during the April to October season.

Close to one corner of the green is the old and spacious parish church; the most remarkable feature is a very unusual staircase in the tower. Shops, inns and restaurants cluster round the green and along the High Street.

Chartwell sits in lovely countryside to the south of Westerham, stately but of modest size, now owned by the National Trust, and full of interest for visitors, particularly those who can remember World War II. Inside, much is as it was during Churchill's occupation, from 1922 until his death in 1965. The exhibits of the history of these times are truly fascinating. The house is set in attractive gardens

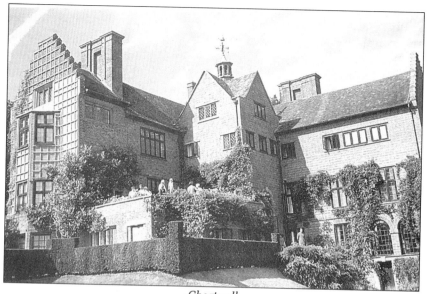

Chartwell

extending to 80 acres, which include water features and Churchill's painting studio. The generous car park is freely available for public use.

Nearby

Emmett's Garden – see walk 2.

Squerryes Court. A 17th-century manor house, family home of the Wardes for over 250 years, beautifully furnished and set in fine gardens, partially restored to the original design of 1709. Open to the public from the beginning of April to the end of September.

The Walk

Leave Westerham High Street along a passageway on the south side, opposite the centre of the triangular green. Descend to cross a stream on a footbridge and go over an old stone stile to reach a gate.

1. Turn right immediately after the gate and follow an obvious path to another gate, crossing a stream on a concrete bridge then join a roadway, with a pond opposite. Turn left, pass an informal parking area, and continue past a house, going over a stile on the right, with a 'Greensand Way' waymark. Rise steadily up a

fenced path between fences, go over a waymarked stile and pass brambles as the gradient eases. Go over another waymarked stile and across a meadow, following 'Greensand Way link'. Go over yet another waymarked stile and through light woodland. At another stile stay with the Greensand Way.

2. Cross a broader track and head into woodland, rising gently. Go straight on at across paths, pass another junction then, at a cross paths with many waymarks, go straight on, following the infallible 'Greensand Way'. Go over a stile beside a small gate; there are more junctions as our Way becomes a narrow path for a short distance. Pass a house on the right, the Way now becoming a broad, surfaced, roadway. At the next cross paths, follow the blue waymark to the left, bearing right at a fork in 20 metres to stay with the major track. Continue uphill through the woods, now on a narrow path. Go straight across a part surfaced driveway, carrying on along the path. Fork right at a waymarked post, pass an informal car parking area with a seat, and go slightly right, then left, on a broad track for a few metres, then turn left to follow a Greensand Way track, rising gently. Pass a house named the Warren, and go along a narrow path, downhill between bracken. There are many paths and many waymarks; stay with the Greensand Way, now quite steeply downhill. Bear right at the bottom to go uphill and join the public road.

3. Cross over Hosey Common Road by a National Trust Mariners Hill sign and go quite steeply uphill on a signposted bridleway. At a waymarked junction the Greensand Way goes off to the left. It has served us well, but we leave it here to go straight on, passing the entrance to Windmill Bank, steadily downhill from the highest part of the route. Join a public road by Garden Cottage, turning left along the roadside for less than 200 metres. Turn right at the Chartwell vehicle exit roadway to descend through the coach park to the National Trust restaurant, shop and the entrance to the house and gardens. Start the return by walking up through the car park, turning left to reach the public road at the Chartwell vehicular entrance.

4. Turn right to walk along the roadside for approximately 200

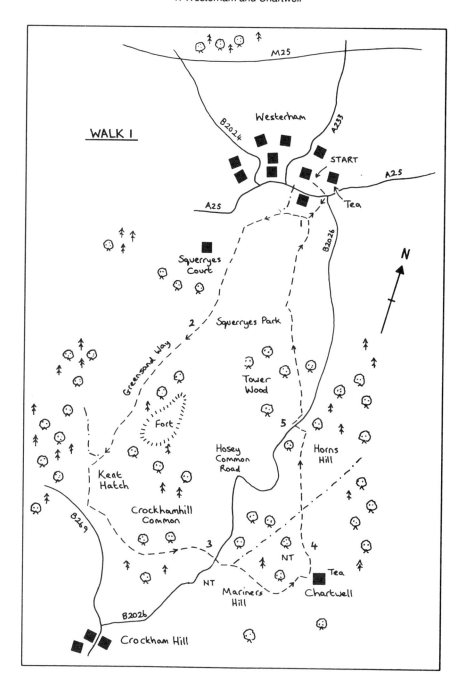

metres. Pass the entrance to Moorcroft Place then, as the road dips to the left, pass the start of a public bridleway and take the next turning on the right, an un-signposted footpath through the trees. Rise steadily up Horns Hill on a good path. At a 'T' junction bear left then right to continue the same line. At a cross paths turn left to return to the public road in 100 metres.

5. Go straight across to a small car parking area, then turn right to follow a signposted footpath descending through woodland, a broad, easy, track. Go straight on at a waymarked junction then go right at the next junction to continue downhill. Turn right, after a waymarked stile, to rise steeply up a grass bank. Follow a track worn across a large meadow, with long views to the North Downs beyond Westerham. Over the brow, Westerham is spread out below. Go through a kissing gate and continue downhill to another kissing gate and rejoin the outward route along the organised path back to the High Street. The recommended tea shop is across the green, to the right. After refreshment, walk along the High Street to the junction with London Road, turning right to descend to the car park.

2. Toy's Hill and Brasted

A good circular walk from the hill top car park, through the National Trust owned woodland of Toy's Hill, descending to Brasted for refreshments before returning to Toy's Hill by a selection of good footpaths. A fair amount of rise and fall – Brasted stands at 90m (295ft) above sea level, Toy's Hill at 245m (804ft) – but, with the exception of a short, sharp, downhill, gradients are never severe. Tracks and paths are uniformly good; almost 1km (two-thirds of a mile) is by the side of a comparatively minor road. Parts of the Greensand Way and the Weardale Walk are included. Waymarking is good, although the profusion of coloured signs on the National Trust land can be confusing. Five stiles.

Distance: 9km (5½ miles).

Start/car parking: Large, free National Trust car park close to the top of Toy's Hill, accessed by the Four Elms to Brasted minor road, grid reference 470517.

Maps: Ordnance Survey Explorer 147, Sevenoaks and Tonbridge, 1:25,000. Ordnance Survey Landranger 188, Maidstone and the Weald, 1:50,000.

Tea Shop

Even on a Sunday when roast lunches are served, walkers wanting just a light snack were welcomed at The Village Tea Room in Brasted. Discretion should be used if boots are muddy as the floor is carpeted; there is a sheltered courtyard but entrance is through the café. The full afternoon tea includes sandwiches or one can choose to have scones with jam and cream. Tempting cakes are date and walnut, lemon drizzle, carrot, and other delicious varieties. Very friendly proprietor and waitress service.

Open: Tuesday to Sunday, 9.30am to 6pm. Tel. 01959 564084.

Introduction

Toy's Hill is the largest of the several National Trust land holdings in the high wooded country to the south of the A25 in the Westerham/Brasted/Sundridge area. It is an area of well-mixed woodland, criss-crossed with waymarked trails. This area has long been associated with Octavia Hill, 19th-century philanthropist and one of the founders of the National Trust.

Brasted is an attractive old village, with tile-hung cottages, inn, tearooms and various shops flanking the fine wide street. The disadvantage is that the A25 main road comprises that village street. The parish church, with 13th-century tower, is on rising ground well to the north west of the village centre.

Nearby

Chartwell (see walk 8).

Emmetts Garden – owned by the National Trust and open to visitors. A lovely hillside garden, with long views across the Weald.

Ide Hill – another wooded hill top owned by the National Trust. The adjacent village has inn, café, car park and public conveniences.

The Walk

From the far end of the car park set off along the right-hand of two inviting tracks, with red, green and orange waymarks. *It has to be said that, to reach point 1 from here, there are several combinations of route. Those who steer a generally northerly course will not go far wrong.* Follow a well-worn track through woodland, a thicket of silver birch in this area. Fork left at a junction in about 100 metres, reaching an open area with a tall memorial stone and long views from the far edge. Continue to a junction with a seat, bearing right to follow the green waymark. Bear right at the next marker post (green waymark), turning left in 40 metres (red waymark). Join a slightly sunken bridleway at a post and turn right to leave the wood, close to a terrace of houses.

1. Join the public road at the edge of Brasted Chart, turning left along the roadside. Pass some houses then, in 30 metres, turn left obliquely into a signposted footpath under trees, narrow but clear. At the bottom go over a waymarked stile, leaving Stanhope Wood, to walk diagonally across a field to a stile. This path is part of the Weardale Walk. Go over another stile with a dog gate, on the left, to descend quite steeply to join an unsurfaced farm access track.

2. Turn right along this track, rising gently and passing through

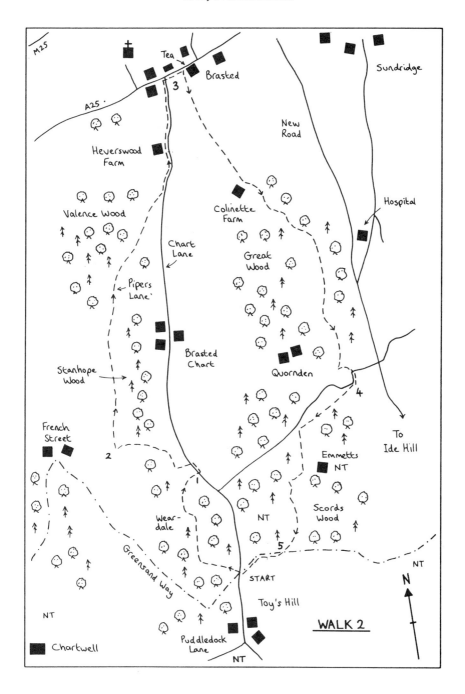

gates to join a surfaced lane. Pass Pipers Green and Piper Farm-house then, as the road turns to the right, go straight on along a 'Byway', the unsurfaced Pipers Lane, heading steadily down-hill, a little horse-churned in places. Join a residential access road, bearing left for 100 metres to reach the public road. Turn left to walk downhill for less than 1km (half a mile) to Brasted, joining the village street by the Kings Arms. *If you find roadside walking too irksome, there is a signposted foot-path which goes up the bank on the left about half way along the road. This joins the main street in Brasted some distance to the west of the centre.* Turn right to reach the tea shop in approximately 150 metres.

The Tea Shop at Brasted

3. Start the return by turning into Elliots Lane, alongside the tea shop, passing charming cottages and footpath signs before following a narrow path between fences, rising to old stone steps and a kissing gate. Pass a junction by a cluster of property and continue along a broad, surfaced, lane. As this lane swings right, into the decrepit Chartfield Farm, go ahead through a waymarked gateway of old railway sleepers. The path is now quite narrow, along the bottom edge of woodland before rising gently into the woodland. Pass another sleeper-built gateway and go straight on at a junction in a few metres, again along the bottom edge of a wood, to a waymarked stile. Pass a donkey

sanctuary, go up a few steps, then rise more steeply to a stile. Go over another stile in 100 metres to join a public road.

4. In 50 metres or so, as the road bends to the right, turn left, through the hedge to a not very obvious waymarked stile. Go over and turn right at once, up a well-worn track, initially close to the entrance drive to Emmetts, the National Trust garden. *To visit the garden, cross over to this drive and walk up through the car park to reach the entrance hut.* Rise steadily between trees and go straight on at a cross tracks. At the next junction the public road is immediately to the right. Bear left here, away from the road, still rising. Pass another cross paths in 200 metres and carry on, now a little downhill. Go left at the next cross paths to rise along a slightly sunken track, now passing through Scords Wood.

5. At the next waymarked cross paths turn right, uphill, now on the Greensand Way. At the next meeting place of tracks, with many waymarks, bear left, still on the Greensand Way, to reach the public road. Cross over to the car park.

3. Penshurst

A varied circuit based on a superb small village, rising over the high ground to Blowers Hill at 103m (338ft), before descending to the valley of the River Medway for a level return to Penshurst. Apart from a short overgrown section, good paths and farm tracks, with less than 1km (two-thirds of a mile) on minor roads. The ascent of the hill is at comparatively gentle gradients. Twelve stiles.

Distance: 7.5km (4¾ miles).

Start/car parking: Roadside layby in Penshurst, close to the public conveniences, grid reference 526439.

Maps: Ordnance Survey Explorer 149, Seveoaks and Tonbridge, 1:25,000. Ordnance Survey Landranger 188, Maidstone and the Weald, 1:50,000.

Tea Shop

Quaintways is exactly the kind of tea shop one would hope to find in Penshurst – certainly quaint, positively attractive, and serving good quality tea including Lapsang, Assam, English breakfast, herbal, and iced tea. Excellent coffee. Good selection of cakes: carrot; chocolate; ginger; lemon; and caramel shortbread. Savouries include old-fashioned favourites such as beans on toast, scrambled egg on toast, or sandwiches. Other items available include filled jacket potatoes and ploughman's lunch. Walkers are welcome but are requested to remove muddy boots.

Open: 10am to 5pm every day all the year but always closed on Mondays. Tel. 01892 870272.

Introduction

Penshurst village is dominated by Penshurst Place, one of England's great privately-owned stately homes. The oldest part of the house dates from 1340-45; extensions and modifications carried out during the ensuing centuries have produced a pleasing mixture of architectural styles. Inside, a wonderful array of furnished rooms, tapestries and works of art is crowned by the majestic Baronial great hall, surviving from the earliest days and widely regarded as the finest medieval hall in the country, the true heart of family life in a

Converted oast house near Penshurst

house of this antiquity. The house has long had royal connections, owned at different times by King Henry VIII and by his son King Edward VI, who gave it to the Sidney family in 1552. It has remained in the ownership of the family since that date. Queen Elizabeth I stayed here, allegedly dancing in the ballroom with her favourite, the 1st Earl of Leicester.

The Place is set in a great expanse of parkland to the north, with 10 acres of walled garden to the south and east. It is open to the public from spring to autumn.

Adjacent to this great focal point, the village clusters close, with its own claims to antiquity, most notably the three-sided Leicester Square, named after the first Earl. The rather better known square of the same name in London was named after the second Earl. Opposite is the Leicester Arms, an absolute jewel of an Elizabethan inn. Along the line of the walk, the local garage has a curious horseshoe-shaped doorway, a relic of the building's former use as a smithy.

Nearby

Chiddingstone is claimed by many to be the prettiest village in Kent. Owned by the National Trust, the village has 16th- and 17th-century houses, and an imitation 'castle' of the 17th century among its attractions.

Near Edenbridge, there is Hever Castle, the childhood home of Anne Boleyn – a great house with wonderful gardens and many treasures to be seen inside. Open to the public from March to November.

The Walk

Walk to the road junction near the recommended tea shop and turn right. Pass the post office/garage/forge stores, with the horseshoe shaped doorway.

1. Opposite a 'public footpath' sign on the left of the road, turn right, into The Warren, by the side of the primary school and follow a surfaced drive, rising gently, soon with pleasing views. Pass a terrace of houses and go through Warren Farm, then over grass to a waymarked stile. Continue along the edge of a field and go over a stile at the bottom; there is a World War II pillbox behind to the right. Proceed over a stile and footbridge in 40 metres, crossing the Medway. Carry on along a fenced section of footpath to a stile, then cross a meadow on a worn path. Go over another stile by a locked gate, then over yet another stile in 100 metres to reach Salman House.

2. Turn right to take a path diversion route along a driveway, soon reaching a private road. Turn left through a kissing gate and continue to another kissing gate in 100 metres. Turn left, up a step, to a third kissing gate and go up the edge of a meadow, with a fence on the left. Go through a kissing gate beside a field gate on the left, then over a stile in 25 metres to follow a field edge path leading to a waymarked stile. Go over and into woodland, cross a plank bridge and turn left along a more major track which, in 30 metres, becomes narrow and somewhat overgrown. Carry on along the edge of the wood, cross a footbridge and bear left to walk along the bottom of a vineyard. Turn right as the woodland ends, cross two little waymarked bridges, and go over a stile. Cross another little stream on a footbridge with stile and follow a track up a rising meadow, heading for trees. Go over a stile and bear left among the trees, still rising, to a flight of steps leading to the public road.

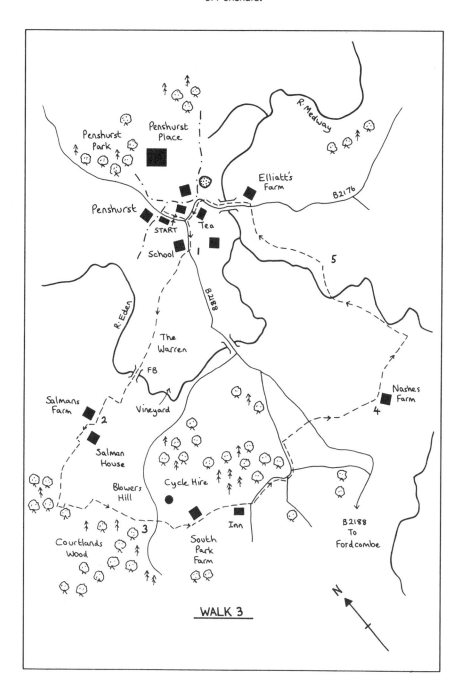

WALK 3

3. Go straight across, up a flight of steps, to continue, soon reaching a large field. Head past an overgrown pond before bearing to the left to a stile which gives access to the South Park Farm access drive. Go along the drive to join a public road by the side of an inn. Turn left to walk by the roadside to a junction. Turn left, then left again at the next junction. Go down the side of this road for about 200 metres then turn right into a signposted bridleway which descends between hedges to reach the main road. Go straight across and follow the signposted bridleway, a broad, unsurfaced lane, to Nashes Farm.

4. Bear left through the farm and continue along a similar track, passing a tiny pond, now very much in the broad, flat, valley of the River Medway. As the lane peters out, by the corner of a hedge, turn left on a footpath, beside a hedge for 20 metres, then bear left diagonally across a cultivated field to reach the bank of the river. Bear right, go over a ditch on a plank bridge, and carry on along a path across a huge field, with isolated great trees, one with a World War II pillbox at its base. Reach the river again, crossing a footbridge. After the bridge, bear left round the edge of a cultivated field, rising to join an old agricultural track.

5. Turn left to walk gently towards Penshurst, nicely elevated above the level of the river. Go up a little rise and the village appears ahead. Join the public road, turning left to cross two bridges and enter the village close by the Penshurst Place entrance lodge. Bear to the left to pass the lovely old houses of Leicester Square and the Leicester Arms Hotel. The tea shop is at the road junction; after refreshment go to the right to return to the parking layby.

4. Tonbridge and Haysden Country Park

An interesting walk, for the most part surprisingly rural considering the proximity to the built-up area of Tonbridge. None of the route is really wild, but there is a good mixture of country park, lakes and the River Medway. Most of the paths, including part of the Eden Valley Walk, are very good, surfaced in some cases, providing easy, level, walking. A particular feature is the number of bridges crossed, well into double figures! One stile.

Distance: 7.5km (4¾ miles).

Start/car parking: Free car park with public conveniences at Haysden Country Park, grid reference 571459. Note: the car park closes at dusk each day and there is a 2m. height restriction.

Maps: Ordnance Survey Explorer 147, Sevenoaks and Tonbridge, 1:25,000. Ordnance Survey Landranger 188, Maidstone and the Weald, 1:50,000.

Tea Shop

The route of the walk passes The Riverside Café at the swimming pool and this is the most suitable place for walkers as it avoids the commercial atmosphere of the town centre. It is very much a family-fun café and serves just about everything including Cola and chips! However, more healthy options are available and there are teatime traditionals such as cakes, toasted teacakes, sandwiches, and, of course, tea and coffee.

Open: Being part of the Leisure Centre the café is open all day every day. Tel. 01732 367449.

Introduction

Tonbridge is a pleasant old town with the remains of a medieval castle set plumb in the middle, by the side of the busy High Street. That street, particularly to the north of the castle, has a great array of 18th-, 19th-century and some older buildings, although the hustle and bustle of the modern town, its shops and commercial property, does to some extent obscure its historic fabric. Beside the castle a

Tonbridge Castle

Victorian cast iron bridge carries the High Street over the River Medway. The gatehouse, used in part as a tourist information centre, is the most substantial surviving part of the castle; the surroundings now comprise landscaped gardens. The famous public school was founded in 1553. The large parish church has some Norman windows in the nave and is partially built on Saxon foundations.

The valley of the Medway to the west of the town has been kept remarkably free of urban and suburban development, no doubt helped by the creation of the Haysden Country Park in recent years. The result is a wide green wedge of open space reaching from the impressive flood barrier to an apex at the castle gardens beside the High Street.

A main feature of the country park is Barden Lake, created in 1974-80 from former gravel workings. Carp, pike and other coarse fish provide sport for anglers and the variety of water-fowl – great crested grebes, mallard, Canada geese, coots and kingfishers among others – is impressive. In season, trips along the river connect the Park with a quay below the castle in the town centre, where boats may also be hired.

Nearby

Royal Tunbridge Wells, the elegant spa town of the 18th and 19th centuries, is a short distance to the south of Tonbridge. Once the claim was made for medicinal properties in local spring water, baths, promenades, fountains and terraces were constructed apace and the town rapidly became extremely fashionable, attracting the great and the good of the time in large numbers. In common with other English spas, in the 20th-century Royal Tunbridge Wells lost its medicinal credibility, but nevertheless the town has retained most of its elegance, adding some modern visitor facilities to the enduring attraction of The Pantiles, The Common and the fine houses.

The Walk

Set off along a broad gravel roadway, with the public conveniences on your right. Go left, under the railway; the lake on the right before the railway is a former ballast pit. The fine Barden Lake, with its wooded island, is reached at once. Bear right to keep the lake on your left, rising a little to pass a slightly elevated 'viewpoint'. The railway is close on the right and there is some exercise equipment along the way.

1. Towards the far end of the lake turn right, over a bridge and through trees. At the far end of the trees turn right to head for 'Barden Park', part of the Tonbridge fringe. A good path goes between hedges, then with allotments on the right. Go straight across the end of a residential road, following a 'footpath' sign. Cross the railway on a high footbridge and carry on along Barden Road. The river, with boat moorings, is soon below to the left, behind the hedge. In about 400 metres turn left, opposite a road junction, to follow a surfaced footpath by the side of the river; across the water there is a children's playground. At a footbridge turn left to cross the water at 'Riverside Walk.', then turn right to continue, with the river now on the right. At the next footbridge cross back and turn left to stay as close as possible to the water. Pass modern council offices and head straight towards the castle. Bear right to reach High Street.

2. Turn left to cross the road bridge and then turn left again at once by the rowing boat landing stage. *To visit the castle and/or the*

T.I.C. detour up to the right. Continue by the riverside for a short distance to a boat landing, bearing right to a signpost, then follow 'Eden Valley Walk'. At the next signpost bear left over a waymarked footbridge. The swimming pool and the café are to the left. Follow the Eden Valley Walk sign outside the swimming pool, keeping the railway coach and the track of the Tonbridge Model Engineering Society to your left. Pass another signpost and go straight on past car parks to a surfaced footpath beside a watercourse. There are playing fields to the left and then to the right. Pass a well-waymarked post and go under the railway. Cross a ditch on a footbridge and walk under trees to a major junction. *A left turn here provides a speedy return to the car park.*

3. Bear right, over a footbridge, to carry on, now close to a lake. Cross a stream on a footbridge to reach a residential area, bearing a little to the left along Powder Mill Lane. Pass a pharmaceutical works and go straight on along a signposted footpath. Join a minor road, walk along the roadside for about 200 metres, then turn left at a 'public footpath' signpost into an unsurfaced roadway, which becomes tree-lined, descending gently after a stile/gate. Pass a crude sign on a tree to the left of the track, cross a bridge, then bear right diagonally across a small field, as indicated by a waymark. The A21, on its viaduct, is now in view as is the Medway flood barrier and its sluices. Pass a waymark on a post, then a footbridge with a few steps on each side and follow a well-worn track across the next field to reach a gate with a stile and a waymark.

4. Do **not** go through; turn sharp left along the edge of the field by the hedge and with a main watercourse on the right. Turn right to cross the watercourse on a bridge, then turn right towards a waymarked gate. Turn left before the gate along the edge of Heusenstamm Friendship Wood. Enter the wood in a few metres, go under the railway and then straight on through a kissing gate at a well-waymarked junction. Go along a narrow path to another kissing gate, cross a watercourse on a footbridge, go left at a 'T' junction then, in a few metres, go round to the right

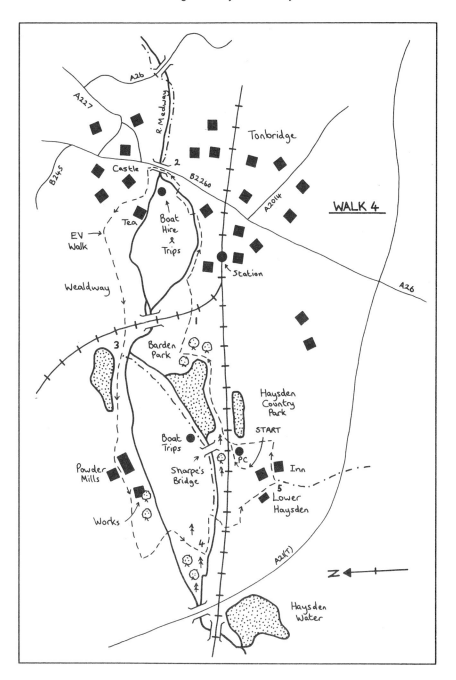

and over another bridge. Bear slightly left after the bridge to walk to a 'bridle route' sign. The track now becomes a lane between hedges as Lower Haysden hamlet comes into view. Go through a gate to join a minor road and reach the hamlet.

5. Bear left in front of the Royal Oak Inn to walk along the public road for 200 metres. Turn left at the entrance to the Country Park to return to the car park.

5. Bewl Water

A walk starting at the small village of Cousley Wood, using minor lanes and tracks to reach the large reservoir at Bewl Water, with its visitor centre. The return route is largely along the shore, a beautiful footpath which is part of the Sussex Border Path. The return includes one quite prolonged ascent, with just a little overgrowth of the path. Otherwise the walking surfaces are first rate. There are no stiles.

Distance: 8.5km (5¼ miles).

Start/car parking: Small free car park at the western end of the Vine Inn at Cousley Wood, grid reference 651334.

Maps: Ordnance Survey Explorer 136, The Weald, 1:25,000. Ordnance Survey Landranger 188, Maidstone and the Weald, 1:50,000.

Tea Shop

Situated at the popular visitor centre, the Look-Out Restaurant is large, efficient and functional. Panoramic windows overlook Bewl Water and there is a sunny terrace along one side of the building. Counter service with just about everything available – coffee and cakes, pizzas and pancakes – salads, sandwiches, and scones – all very enjoyable during a pleasant walk.

Open: April (or Easter if earlier) to end of October 10.30am to 5.30pm. Other months open weekends only 10.30am to 4pm or dusk. Tel. 01892 890171.

Introduction

At nearly 4 miles long, Bewl Water is the largest and most impressive sheet of inland water in the south east. Created as a reservoir in 1973-75 by Southern Water, it has all the beauty of a natural lake. The well-wooded shores include a great deal of silver birch, oak and conifers, with bramble undergrowth. There are waterfowl and squirrels in profusion. The addition of a visitor centre, picnic area, sailing, rowing and fishing activities adds up to a comprehensive visitor attraction without detracting significantly from the natural beauty.

The visitor centre itself has an informative display, plus a shop

Bewl Water Visitor Centre

and café, with cycle hire, wind surfing and, in season, boat trips all close by. The large car park is quite expensive to use.

Cousley Wood is a quiet little place astride the B2100, with the Vine Inn as its only notable feature.

The Walk

Start by crossing the main road in Cousley Wood to follow the minor road opposite the car park. In less than 50 metres turn right by a part tile hung house into a very minor lane. At a 'T' junction go straight ahead along a narrow track between hedges, to reach another minor lane. Turn right, shortly passing a crossroads, going straight on to follow the 'Lamberhurst' sign.

1. Cross the main road and proceed along the lane opposite, passing Ladymeads Farm, then go straight on at the junction by the Hook Farm entrance drive. Pass a vehicular barrier; a sailing dinghy park is visible through the hedge on the right. Turn right, through double wooden gates, then fork left in 50 metres along a wide tarmac roadway. Ignore a right turn, pass an overflow car parking area on the left, then bear right to descend to the visitor centre.

2. From the car park above the visitor centre, head for woodland on

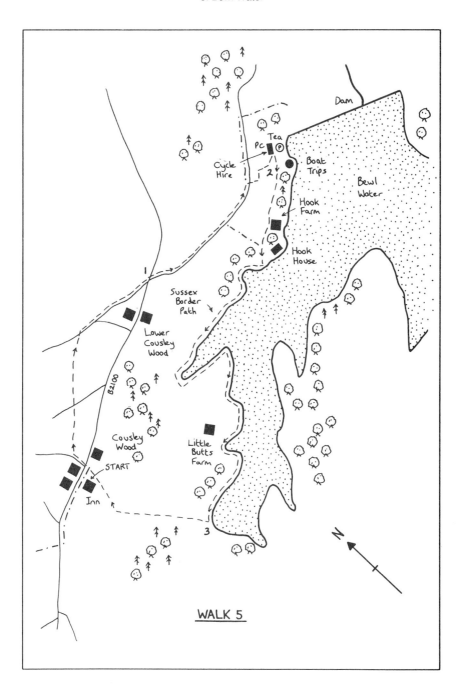

WALK 5

a wide, surfaced, path. Pass through the woodland, cross a surfaced roadway, and follow a signpost 'round Bewl Water walk', soon reaching another surfaced road giving access to Bewl Bridge Rowing Club. Pass the clubhouse and a large boat storage area before turning left, back into woodland, at a signpost. Go down a short flight of steps and then up a shorter flight to join a very minor lane. Head for the water, go through a gate, with a warning of the 13-mile distance of a full circuit of the reservoir, and turn right along a broad woodland track. Emerge from the woodland on a grassy bank above the lake shore. Continue along this fine path, with an uphill turn along a wide section, then a return to the lake shore. Cross a tiny stream on a bridge then pass a vineyard on the right.

3. By the far end of the lake, as the track bends to the left, look carefully for a right turn. At the far apex of a triangle of grass which has no obvious path there is a small gate with a 'Cousley Wood ¾ mile' sign. Go through and ascend the hillside on a lightly trodden footpath at the left-hand edge of rough grassland. Although a little overgrown in places, the path is not difficult to follow. At the top of the hill bear right as the track improves considerably, then join a surfaced driveway leading to Little Butts Farm. Turn left along the drive to rise to Cousley Wood village and the car park.

6. Lamberhurst and Owl House

A circular walk in attractive countryside, woodland and agricultural, linking one of England's most celebrated vineyards with a fine garden open to the public. The paths and tracks are generally good; some are very good. Roadside walking totals about 450 metres on minor roads and 50 metres on a main road. The route has a fair amount of rise and fall, but none of the gradients are steep. There are nine stiles.

Distance: 7km (4¼ miles).

Start/car parking: As customers of the vineyard tea room, use of the spacious car park is permitted, grid reference 672357. The car park is accessed from the B2169, Lamberhurst to Tunbridge Wells road.

Maps: Ordnance Survey Explorer 136, The Weald, 1:25,000. Ordnance Survey Landranger 188, Maidstone and the Weald, 1:50,000.

Tea Shop

Resist the temptation to visit the vineyard shop and tea room until after the walk! However, the venue is very appropriate for morning coffee, light lunch, or afternoon tea – a farmhouse version is available which includes scones with cream or try the warm cheese variety; cakes and sandwiches are also available. A speciality is the treacle tart, served warm with fresh cream. Tea and coffee is of excellent quality; decaffeinated coffee and fruit teas are also on offer. The shop has tasteful gift items but the main interest is the wine, produced on the premises and at other vineyards in Kent. Tasting and purchase available at all times except Sunday mornings.

If looking for more substantial meals, and a quite different atmosphere, visit 'The Swan at The Vineyard' which is under the same ownership, situated at the top of the car park.

Open: 10am to 5pm every day. Tel. 01892 890412.

Introduction

Once a centre of the long defunct iron industry of the Weald, Lamberhurst is now, apart from the busy A21 main road, a quiet village in a deep valley close to the Sussex border, with old cottages, a few shops, inns and an interesting old church. Most famous of the

The tea room at Lamberhurst Vineyard

products of the former Lamberhurst iron industry were the railings which surrounded St. Paul's cathedral in London for many years.

The comparatively large vineyard dates from 1972, well to the forefront of the revival of wine production in this country; Lamberhurst remains one of the most famous names in English wine. Visitors are welcomed for tours of the vineyard, tasting, purchases from the well-equipped shop and refreshments in the tea room or the adjacent Swan at the Vineyard Inn.

At Owl House, on the route of this walk, there are 13 acres of lovely gardens, including beautiful water features and woodland, open to the public throughout the year. The house itself, a 16th-century former wool smugglers' cottage, remains private.

Nearby

The ruins of Baynham Abbey, in the bottom of the valley of the River Teise, are close to Lamberhurst. In the care of English Heritage, they are open to the public from spring to autumn.

Scotney Castle Gardens (National Trust) are also close by – see walk 7.

The Walk

Leave the vineyard car park by heading north, passing the shop on the right and a large building occupied by a fencing firm, Stenoak house, on the left. Go through a small apple orchard, reaching a broad track in a short distance.

1. Turn left to follow this track, with splendid views across the valley, passing vineyards to right and left. Go through a gate with a 'public footpath' sign and continue. On reaching trees at the far end, turn right, then immediately left, down a few steps to a concrete track. Turn right to descend the valley side, between hedges. Cross the mini river on a bridge and carry on up the track, forking right in less than 100 metres along a grass path, initially through bracken, then a sunken lane between high hedges. Go through two field gates, rising along the edge of a field, with woodland on the left. At the top of the rise go through an open gate to join a very minor road. Turn left along the roadside for 150 metres.

2. Turn right along a surfaced drive towards Owl House Gardens, passing the extensive apple orchards of Owlett Farm. Pass the farm, then the entrance gate to Owl House Gardens, guarded by a stone owl. Continue to a small gate on the left in 80 metres, turning left here to follow a path along the edge of the wood to a waymarked stile in less than 100 metres. Pass through the wood on a well-defined path. Leave the wood at a waymarked post, descending through a forest of willow herb and down a steep little bank to approach a ruinous cottage. Bear left in front of this building and then round to the right before going to the left to cross a small open space, downhill, entering woodland, where the track becomes much more apparent. Rise through woodland, under power lines, turning right at a junction by an electricity pylon, now heading between the trees towards a building with oast house (Lindridge Oast) on the hill ahead. Descend to a farm pond, go through a gate and rise steadily along the middle of a huge meadow, towards the farm at the top. There is no real path. Go through a field gate and rise to the right along the farm drive to join the A21 main road. Turn right to walk on the grass verge for 50 metres.

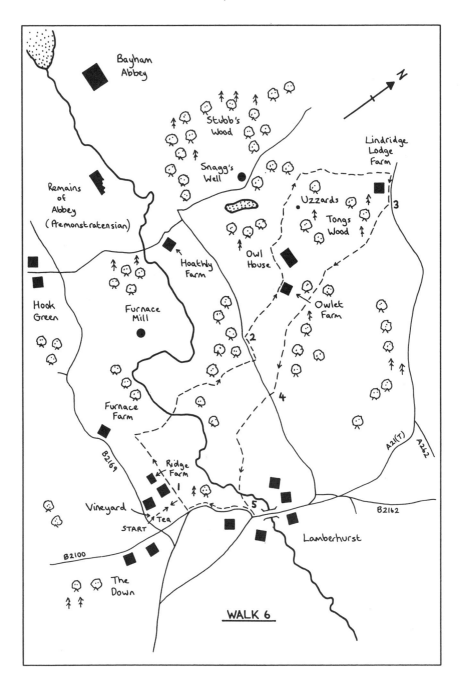

Bayham
Abbey

Stubb's
Wood

Snagg's
Well

Lindridge
Lodge
Farm

3

Uzzards

Tongs
Wood

Remains
of
Abbey
(Premonstratensian)

Hoathly
Farm

Owl
House

2

Owlet
Farm

Hook
Green

Furnace
Mill

4

Furnace
Farm

A21(T)

A262

B2169

Ridge
Farm

1

Vineyard

5

Tea

START

B2162

B2100

Lamberhurst

The
Down

WALK 6

3. Turn right at a 'public footpath' signpost, go over a stile and along a grass lane, passing derelict farm buildings. Go over a waymarked stile and continue through woodland. At an open area bear left then right to carry on, with a hedge on the left and bramble to the right. Bear right, then fork left to stay close to the field boundary, going over a waymarked stile in a further 50 metres; there are now long views to the left. Go gently downhill to another stile, then along the edge of a field, before turning left over a waymarked stile close to two field gates. We are now in the woodland part of the Owl House Gardens. Fork left in 40 metres and bear right to reach an ornamental pathway. Turn right to pass two stone seats and an owl on a pedestal. Turn left in 20 metres at a 'willow pond' sign and go through more woodland, soon forking right to approach the very pretty willow pond. Just after passing a seat, turn left, then bear to the right to a waymarked stile. After the stile keep left to pass a tennis court and follow a path along the edge of woodland, soon with an orchard on the right. Reach farm buildings and go up the drive, to a minor road.

4. Turn left for 5 metres and then turn right, through a farm gate, with a traditional concrete 'public footpath' sign; there is soon a good 'surprise view'. Go straight on, descending a long slope on a grass path, between fields; Lamberhurst is in view, below to the left. Reach the end of a hedge and keep right. As another hedge joins from the right, turn left, diagonally across a field, heading for an agricultural building. Join a farm track at the bottom, turning left. In 20 metres turn right, through the hedge to a waymarked stile. Continue through a meadow on a worn path, crossing the valley bottom towards Lamberhurst village. Go over a stile, cross a bridge, then a second bridge, to follow the path through a garden, reaching a stony track and then the village street.

5. Turn right to walk uphill on the roadside pavement, passing the Baptist Chapel. Just before a road junction on the left, turn right, up a few steps, (concrete footpath sign) to walk along the vineyard track for almost 200 metres before turning left to retrace the outward route back to the vineyard car park.

7. Goudhurst

A varied ramble through charming Wealden countryside to the south of Goudhurst, all on good tracks and footpaths with less than 1km (3/4 mile) on predominantly quiet roadsides. The return to Goudhurst involves a steady ascent of about 70 metres (230ft). Eleven stiles.

Distance: 4.5km (2¾ miles).

Start/car parking: Small free car park with public conveniences close to the crossroads in Goudhurst, accessed from the B2079, grid reference 722377.

Maps: Ordnance Survey Explorer 136, The Weald, 1:25,000. Ordnance Survey Landranger 188, Maidstone and the Weald, 1:50,000.

Tea Shop

As we were staying near to Goudhurst for a long period, we wanted to include this walk but found that the only tea shop had recently closed down. However, Weeks, the bakers, provide Britannia style tables and chairs outside the shop and sell tea, coffee, cakes, scones, hot or cold savouries, and sandwiches – quite satisfactory on a good day. Otherwise try the 'Star and Eagle' further up the hill, for coffee, drinks, and pub-style food.

Introduction

Climbing up the side of a hill, in an area where orchards and hop gardens abound, Goudhurst is one of the most attractively situated villages of the High Weald. The main street rises inevitably towards the church where, from the tower of 1638, the views are immense on a clear day, Hastings and similarly distant places being within range. Inside the church the most notable feature is the collection of monuments to the Culpeppers, one of the great Kent families of the middle ages. Many of the buildings lining the main street are very fine, now serving as shops and inns. The small duckpond and its grass surround provide a tranquil area close to the crossroads.

Nearby

Scotney Castle Gardens, set around the ruin of a moated 14th-century castle, are owned by the National Trust. There is access to the gardens during the season and unrestricted access to the adjacent area of countryside, including woodland, throughout the year.

Finchcocks, even closer to Goudhurst, houses the Living Museum of Music, a comprehensive collection of keyboard instruments, together with some mechanical musical devices. The house is an early Georgian (1725) manor in a very pleasant setting, including parkland at the front and a restored garden at the rear. Public admission is restricted to the afternoons on specified days of the week during the summer season only.

Goudhurst

The Walk

Leave the car park by crossing the road and following a minor road opposite. Pass a few houses and then turn sharp right, downhill, at a road junction, with long views to the left. On approaching the main road, turn left, downhill, into a surfaced roadway with a 'public footpath' signpost. Pass a few houses and an equine establishment, then a small development of 'executive' houses. Carry on along the waymarked High Weald Landscape Trail, now an unsurfaced lane.

1. In 150 metres or so after passing the houses, go left at a waymarked fork and keep close to the hedge on the left, still descending. At the bottom bear slightly right to a well-made wooden footbridge over a stream. There is a stile at each end of the bridge. Continue on a footpath across a rising meadow, often alive with pheasants, to reach a farm track with a waymark on a post. Turn right, along this track; Goudhurst can be seen on its hilltop to the right. Head for the large Smugley farmstead, going through the farm across a concrete surfaced area, turning left to descend gently on a broad track after passing most of the farm buildings. There is a large converted oast house 100 metres to the right. Turn right at the bottom, with the trackbed of the former Paddock Wood to Hawkhurst railway line close on the left. Converge with a surfaced farm access road, but bear left to leave it immediately along a waymarked rough path, heading for trees and a stile. Continue to another stile, cross a paddock, and go over another stile to join a public road.

2. Cross over the road, go through a waymarked gate, descend steps, cross a plank bridge over a stream, go over another stile and along the edge of a meadow to two sets of waymarked gates. Follow the indicated line across the middle of a large field. Most fields hereabouts seem to be in equestrian use. Go through a field gate and immediately turn right through another gate to head for a small wood. Keep to the left of the wood to reach a signposted stile and a surfaced lane. Turn left along the lane, pass the entrance to Risebridge Farm and turn right at a road junction to head uphill towards Goudhurst. Pass Ranter's Hall, a site used by the adherents of a peculiar form of 17th-century Christianity, on the left and then Thatcher's on the right.

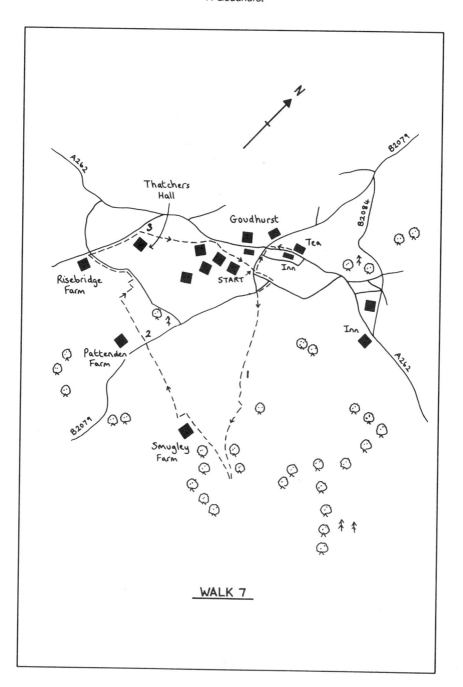

WALK 7

3. Turn right at a 'public footpath' sign, along a narrow path between hedges to a stile, then across a paddock to the next stile, rising gently with Wealden views to the right and to Goudhurst ahead. Go over a stile at the top of the field and follow a little path into a residential area. Cross an estate road, bearing left to the main road. Turn right, uphill then, in 20 metres turn right into an unsurfaced roadway. In 10 metres turn left along a path which goes through a house garden, leading to a stile in 40 metres. Carry on along what appears to be an old lane between hedges, soon encroached upon by house construction over the years. Go through a little gate and then a second gate, reaching the end of a tarmac roadway. Go ahead along the roadway to return direct to the car park. For the village street, and refreshments, continue up past the car park and turn right at the crossroads.

8. Cranbrook and Sissinghurst

A pleasant country walk in the form of a figure 8, based on the small town of Cranbrook and the National Trust Sissinghurst Castle and Gardens. At the crossover point is Sissinghurst village. The route includes a good deal of agricultural land and woodland, over a mixture of tracks and footpaths, with just a little roadside walking. Part of the High Weald Landscape Trail is included. Nine stiles, well-distributed throughout the walk. Obviously, either part of the figure 8 can be treated as a separate walk.

Distance: 11.5km (7¼ miles).

Start/car park Large free car park with public conveniences behind High Street in Cranbrook, grid reference 775359.

Maps: Ordnance Survey Explorer 136, The Weald, 1:25,000 (most of the route). Ordnance Survey Explorer 137, Ashford (part of the route). Ordnance Survey Landranger 188, Maidstone and the Weald, 1:50,000.

Tea Shop

The restaurant at Sissinghurst Castle, known as The Granary, is the chosen eatery for part way round this walk. The building, decor, and the menu are all most attractive. The well-deserved refreshments will no doubt take priority but if time permits, the gardens are wonderful. The menu is 'all day' – savoury main courses might include Kentish lamb with cherries, Appledore chicken pie, ploughman's lunch, or a vegetarian flan. To go with coffee, or a pot of tea, there are temptations such as banana bread, raspberry bread, and even courgette bread, all served with butter. Cakes available include ginger and pineapple or marmalade as well as more usual varieties such as jam sponge or chocolate. The home-made lemonade is excellent. Decaffeinated coffee and fruit teas are available. The tables near to the picture windows benefit from views across the Weald of Kent.

Open: 1st April (or Easter if earlier) to 15th October on Tuesday to Friday, 12 to 5.30pm and on Saturday, Sunday and Good Friday, 10am to 5pm. From mid October to 22nd December (approx.) open on

Wednesday to Sunday. To confirm opening hours out of the main season, please telephone 01580 710704.

Cranbrook

Introduction

Situated among gentle hills by the headwaters of the River Crane, Cranbrook is a pleasant small town, its High Street lined with good buildings, with the traditional weatherboarding prominent. Perhaps even more prominent is the seven-storey Union Mill, claimed to be the tallest working windmill in England, built in 1814 by a local millwright. The mill worked until 1958, when it was taken over by Kent County Council and fully restored. There are now open days for the public during the summer season, when the mill is again wind operated, grinding flour for sale in the mill shop.

The town was granted a market charter late in the 13th century, later enjoying a wool engendered prosperity from the 14th to the 16th centuries. From the 17th century onwards Cranbrook became a centre for local agriculture. The subsequent decline in wealth has fortuitously resulted in a high proportion of old buildings remaining intact rather than being replaced, hence the good array of old Wealden structures and the medieval layout of streets and alleys.

St Dunstan's church of the 14th to 16th centuries, the 'Cathedral of the Weald', stands on a raised site close to the town centre, a fine 'wool' church reminiscent of several in the Cotswolds. The site had earlier Saxon and Norman structures. The mechanism of the church clock was the prototype for 'Big Ben'. A local museum is housed in a building of 1480 in Carriers Road. As would be expected, there are plenty of shops and inns and a tourist information centre occupying part of the former Vestry Hall.

Sissinghurst is an altogether more modest place, a village bisected by the busy A262 but with some good traditional buildings, a handful of shops and the Bull Inn. Sissinghurst Castle (National Trust) is a Tudor building with lovely gardens originally laid out by Vita Sackville-West, open to visitors during the normal National Trust season. The complex also includes other attractions, not least the splendid tea room.

The Walk

From the car park walk downhill towards the town centre, pass the public conveniences and turn left to reach the High Street. Turn right for a short distance and then turn left by the T.I.C. to follow the path across the churchyard, keeping to the left of the church. Leave the churchyard, bearing right along a surfaced path, between a childrens' play area and the churchyard wall. The route soon becomes a lightly worn path along the edge of a large playing field. Keep to the right as the path forks after passing the play area Go down a few steps, cross a road and go up a few steps on the far side, by a 'footpath to Sissinghurst' signpost. Go over a waymarked stile in 60 metres to follow an excellent path, with well-protected parkland to the left.

1. Turn right at a waymarked field gate/stile to continue along a grass track reserved between cultivated fields, part of the High Weald Landscape Trail. At the edge of woodland turn right; then, in 100 metres, turn left to go slightly downhill to more woodland, going straight ahead to pass a tiny pond and cross a stream on a bridge. Carry on along the edge of another field, then go left and right at a waymarked tree belt and cross another smaller field to join a public road, over a stile. Go over and turn left along the roadside for 75 metres.

2. Fork right at Coursehorn Lane; there is a concrete 'public footpath' sign. Follow the lane, rising very gently and bearing to the left at a junction, soon passing the entrance to Dulwich Primary School. Leave the surfaced roadway here by going straight on, with a duckpond on the right, passing the various buildings of Coursehorn Farm. Opposite the last and biggest of these buildings, leave the concrete track by forking left along a footpath trodden across a huge arable field, descending gently, aiming for a lone tree, then the end of a tree-lined ditch. Keep to the right of the ditch, pass through an old gateway and turn left on joining a track among the trees. Rise to join the public road at the hamlet of Golford.

3. Turn right, then left at the crossroads in less than 100 metres, following the 'Sissinghurst' sign. Walk by the roadside for about 300 metres then turn left over a stile at a 'footpath' signpost. Follow the indicated direction to the left, towards a waymarked gate. Take care to turn right as indicated before the tree-lined ditch. Continue close to the ditch to reach a stile and enter woodland. Cross a little stream on a footbridge and bear right, along a woodland path, soon going to the left, up a low bank to reach another bridge. Stay with the path through the wood before emerging into a very large rising field, with a wide grass path up the middle; the buildings at the edge of Sissinghurst are in view ahead. Go under trees and keep straight on at a crossing of paths to reach the village street (A262). Turn right to pass the Bull Inn and the church, continuing by the roadside for a further 200 metres towards Biddenden.

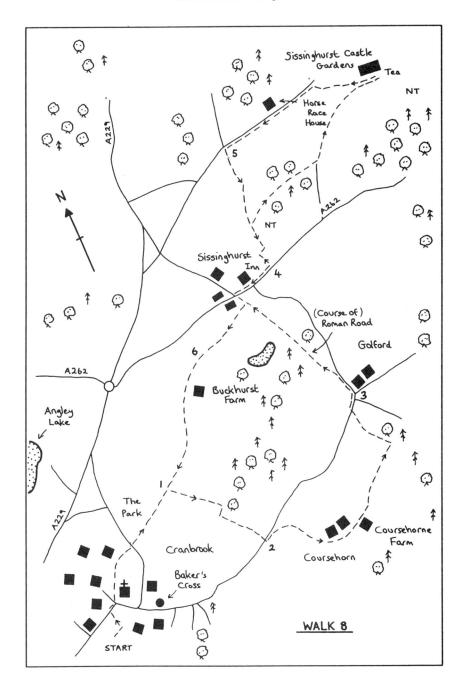

4. Turn left at a wide track, signposted by the National Trust to 'Sissinghurst Garden, cross country route, ¾ mile'. Follow this track, soon descending quite steeply. Fork left by the entrance to the sewage works and carry on along the edge of a hop garden. Cross a stream on a footbridge and then turn right at a little gate with a 'Sissinghurst Garden' signpost. Stay with the excellent trail, provided by the National Trust, through beech, silver birch and oak woodland. On reaching the drive to Sissinghurst Castle turn left to walk up to the complex, following the signs to the Granary Restaurant. To return to the village, follow the yellow waymarks through the various car parking areas, eventually reaching a stile at the far right extremity. Go over and turn right for a few metres to reach an unsurfaced lane in front of a house. Turn left along the lane, soon passing Horse Race House.

5. On approaching a minor road, turn left immediately before the road, going over a stile to descend along a wide track through a huge apple orchard. Look out carefully for yellow waymarks, angling across the orchard towards the right-hand boundary, then descending to and through the edge of the wood to rejoin the outward route just before the footbridge. Return to Sissinghurst village past point 4, keeping to the outward route as far as the cross paths which is reached soon after leaving the main street. Turn right here, along a good path, initially under trees but soon reaching more open country.

6. Descend a few steps to cross the Buckhurst Farm access drive and then go up a few steps on the far side and over a stile. Continue straight across a field, with the farm in view below to the left. Go over a stile at the bottom of the field and enter woodland, rising steadily. At the top of the wood carry on along a roughly concreted farm track, with a hedge on the right and Union Mill in view ahead. Rejoin the outward route by the gate at point 1 and retrace the route into Cranbrook.

9. Biddenden and Goose Green

A gentle level walk in the countryside around Biddenden, a village of great charm, passing the hamlet of Goose Green. Good footpaths, one field to cross and 1km (two-thirds of a mile) on a surfaced lane. Fine preparation for enjoying the refreshments at Claris's. Eleven stiles.

Distance: 4.5km (2¾ miles).

Start/car parking: Small free car park with public conveniences beside the small green at the village centre, grid reference 851383.

Maps: Ordnance Survey Explorer 137, Ashford, 1:25,000. Ordnance Survey Landranger 188, Maidstone and the Weald (most). Ordnance Survey Landranger 189, Ashford and Romney Marsh (a little), 1:50,000.

Tea Shop

Claris's is very well known – it features in various guides and enjoys a reputation as a typical English tea shop. It is quite 'genteel' with a well-carpeted floor. However, walkers are indeed welcome here but it might be preferable to make a brief visit to the car to deposit rucksacks and boots before enjoying the ambience of this delightful café. Temptations abound including meringues with fresh cream, Victoria sponge cake, excellent scones, and toasted teacakes. Savouries offered include creamed mushrooms or poached eggs both served on toast; or a choice of sandwiches. Very good coffee is served and there is a selection of blends of tea.

Open: Tuesday to Sunday 10.30am – 5pm. Tel. 01580 291025.

Introduction

Biddenden's little village street is a real gem, leading from the green to the church as a village street should, with timber-framed buildings overhanging the pavement. Particularly good is the former Old Cloth Hall, a complex building with no less than seven gables. All Saints Church is a great sprawling structure, with a particularly well-made roof to the high nave. The Tudor font is on short, slightly incongruous legs; more notable is the rich array of brasses commemorating eminent local people. For nine hundred years the village has been known as the home of Eliza and Mary Chulkhurst, the

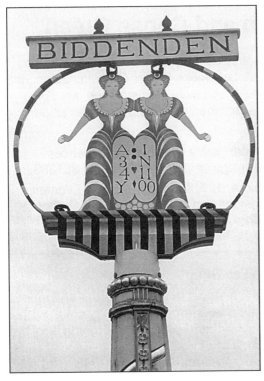

The Biddenden "Maydes"

'Biddenden Maids' believed to have lived here as Siamese twins until their death at 34 years old in 1100. Many gravestones are fashioned in a 'Siamese twin' shape and there has long been an appropriate village sign on the green, which won a prize in a competition in the 1920s. The present sign is a refurbishment of 1993. Allegedly from a bequest made on the death of the sisters, bread, cheese and biscuits bearing the imprint of Siamese twins are distributed on the morning of Easter Monday each year. Apparently, even visitors to the village qualify for this benevolence. The village has shops, including antiques, inns and restaurants.

Goose Green is nothing more than a tiny hamlet.

Nearby

Biddenden Vineyard, long established and welcoming visitors.

Headcorn has a charming village centre, surrounded by a great deal of modern housing development.

The Walk

Turn left from the car park, pass the green with the village sign and the tea shop, to walk along the remarkable village street to All Saints Church. Go through the Lych Gate and take the path to the right of the church. Continue along a footpath, cross a residential road, then a tiny stream on a footbridge. Turn right immediately; this section of path has wooden edging and a hedge on the right. Bear left to pass a children's play area, then right to go through a gap in a hedge, reaching a stile in a further 40 metres. Follow a well-worn path across a rough meadow to a waymarked stile by a little pond. Bear left to another stile in 50 metres. In 20 metres fork left to follow a good path across a large field; go over a plank bridge and a double stile at the far end of the field. Cross a rough meadow, heading for a waymarked post, pass a silted pond with luxuriant vegetation, then aim for another marked post beside an overgrown watercourse.

1. At this point do **not** pass the post, but turn left to walk beside the watercourse for a few metres before continuing the same line across the field towards a barely visible stile. If the grass is uncomfortably long, walk around the right-hand boundary. Go over a waymarked double stile and proceed along the left-hand edge of a field, bearing left under trees in a corner by another little pond. Go over a stile and along a fenced path, reaching the A262 main road over a stile at the hamlet of Worsenden Green. Go straight across to follow the surfaced lane opposite, passing Worsenden Farm. *(A signposted footpath on the left provides a short cut back to Biddesden, if required)*; the church tower is in view. Pass Randolph Lodge, a farmhouse with a former oast house behind. Pass High Poles Farm, as the hamlet of Goose Green is reached.

2. After passing Victory Cottage, turn left in a few metres along a signposted, rough surfaced bridleway leading to Goose Cottage. The surface is lost after passing the last house. Carry on, partly under trees, to a well-waymarked post. Turn left here to follow the yellow waymark, over a stile then along a path at the left-hand edge of a field, slightly downhill and with impressive oaks on the right. Go over a waymarked stile at the bottom, pass a small pond, and keep to the bottom edge of another field. Cross another stile, under trees and cross the tiniest of streams on a plank bridge. Emerge from the trees at a marker post in about 50 metres, turning right to rise by the side of a hedge; there are good long views here, including the church tower. There are also a

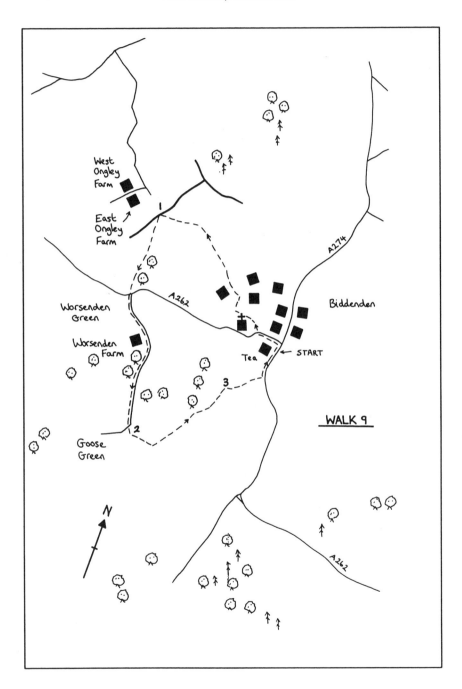

seat and a modern, Biddesden 2000, orientation table, with directions to various European cities and a few local places. In the distance are two standing and one horizontal large stones.

3. Go through a kissing gate on the right and head across the well-tended recreation ground, passing a seat and aiming to the right of the large pavilion building. Leave the recreation ground by the access roadway, join the A262, and turn left along the roadside path to return to the tea shop and the car park.

10. Tenterden and Rolvenden

A circuit connecting the very pleasant little town of Tenterden with the spacious village of Rolvenden, mainly across agricultural land, with less than the average proportion of woodland. There is only a modest amount of rise and fall, with the odd short, steep, section as the route crosses a shallow valley, and the line of the preserved Kent and East Sussex Railway. Underfoot are some good tracks, one rough path, some cultivated fields, 1km (two-thirds of a mile) of minor road and village street, and part of the High Street in Tenterden. Thirteen stiles.

Distance: 9.5km (6 miles).

Start/car parking: The main street in Rolvenden is wide, with the occasional layby, and appears to be generally used for car parking; typical grid reference 844315.

Maps: Ordnance Survey Explorer 125, Romney Marsh, 1:25,000. Ordnance Survey Landranger 189, Ashford and Romney Marsh, 1:50,000.

Tea Shop

There are many tea shops to choose from in charming, sophisticated, Tenterden. Just opposite the War Memorial, on the left approaching the town from the Rolvenden direction, is Porters Coffee House and Antique Shop. Here are tables on the pavement under the sun blind, very much in the continental style, and one can observe passers-by whilst enjoying refreshment. The selection of coffees include Espresso and Machiatto, teas include Darjeeling, Lapsang, or fruit. Perhaps for a change from scones and cakes for tea, try the Danish pastries or pain au chocolat. If visiting for lunch, the menu includes quiche with salad, or paté, salad, and a basket of fresh bread. The indoor tearoom is most attractive but not really appropriate for 'boots'.

Open: 8.30am to 5.30pm every day but always closed on Sundays. Tel. 01580 766696.

Introduction

The pleasantly unpretentious village of Rolvenden has a wide main street, a few shops and inns and a 13th/14th-century church. The railway station, part of the preserved Kent and East Sussex line, is no less than 2.5km (1½ miles) by road from the village which it ostensibly served. Also in Rolvenden is the C.M. Booth collection of historic motor vehicles, particularly strong on three-wheel Morgans.

The Kent and East Sussex Railway is operated as a mainly steam-hauled (summer season and main holidays) preserved line. Originally a 'Col. Stephens' light railway built to serve a lightly populated area neglected by the major companies of the 19th century, it is hard to imagine that the line was ever profitable. It was closed as early as 1953. As reconstituted, it is now a considerable visitor attraction, offering a seven mile ride from Tenterden to Northiam, using a variety of historic rolling stock. The

Signal box on the Kent and East Sussex Railway

station area at Tenterden has a signal box, museum, refreshments, gift shop and a large car park. At Rolvenden station, on the line of this walk, is the locomotive depot, with a public viewing platform.

Tenterden is a most attractive small town with a wide, elegant, High Street abounding in lovely historic houses, many being of the 15th and 16th centuries, in some cases the timber framing being concealed by later tile hanging. Antique shops, inns and tea rooms cluster along the sides of this fine street, occupying many of the historic houses. Close behind is the church, long famed for its great pinnacled tower, with weather vanes at each corner. In Station Road the Tenterden and District Museum displays local history, including agriculture and the Cinque Ports.

Nearby

Close to Rolvenden is Great Maytham Hall; in the grounds is the walled garden which inspired Frances Hodgson Burnett's novel 'The Secret Garden'.

The Walk

Walk along the main street in Rolvenden, passing the junction with the B2086 and the motor museum.

1. Cross the road and then turn left to take a grass surfaced path at a 'public footpath' sign 100 metres before the speed de-restriction sign. Go through a field gate and bear to the right across the field, passing close to the corner of a hedge, to reach a stile in the bottom corner. Go over and then turn left along a surfaced lane. Almost opposite Halden Lane Farm turn right, along a sign-posted footpath, cross a plank bridge, go over a waymarked stile and continue along the top edge of a field, initially with woodland on the left. As the woodland ends, keep the same line to a waymarked stile. Go over, and through a narrow tongue of woodland, leaving the wood over a waymarked stile in 40 metres. Carry on along the edge of a meadow, approaching Little Halden Farm. Go through a waymarked field gate, turn left in 20 metres through an open gate, then turn right immediately to head for another open gate in 50 metres. Turn left to stay beside the fence on the left as far as an old field gate at the bottom. Head for the corner of a hop garden.

2. Turn right, along an agricultural track, through a gate and along the bottom of the hop garden, with a watercourse on the left. Turn left to cross the water on a footbridge with stile, then turn right in 15 metres at a waymarked post, on a rough path along the top edge of a large field, close to a fence on the left; pheasants are plentiful hereabouts. Go over two waymarked stiles and

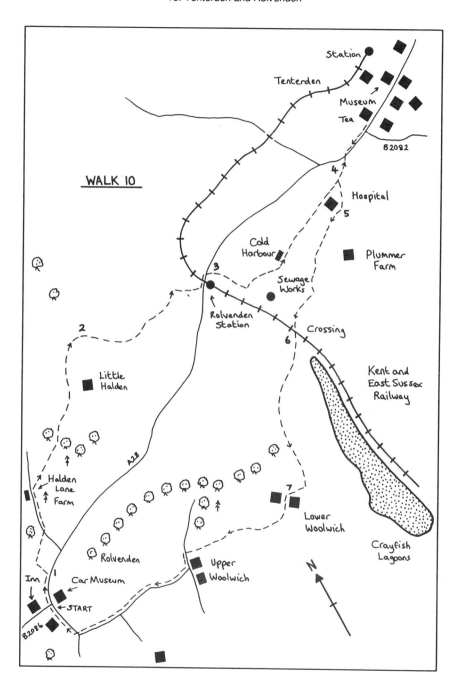

WALK 10

keep the same line towards the now visible railway line. Go over a waymarked stile on the left in 100 metres and stay close to the fence on the right. Go through a field gate on the right and walk to the public road in 100 metres. Turn left by the roadside, over the level crossing; a short diversion along the station platform leads to the public viewing gallery by the locomotive depot. Continue along the roadside.

3. Turn right in 70 metres at a 'public footpath' sign, over a cattle grid and along a concrete roadway. Before the entrance to the sewage works turn left, go through a waymarked field gate and rise quite steeply on a broad track. Go through a field gate and on to Cold Harbour Farm. Follow the waymarks through the farm buildings, being prepared for a possible diversion. Carry on along the concrete farm access drive, passing below the back of West View Hospital. At a junction with a tarmac roadway, go left to rise to the A28 main road; across the road is Westwell Spring, an old water supply restored in 1984.

4. Turn right to walk into the middle of Tenterden. The recommended tea shop is on the left as the shopping area is reached. *(The Kent and East Sussex railway station and the museum are found by walking further along the High Street, then turning left at Station Road).* From the tea shop turn right to retrace the route along the High Street, turning left at point 4. towards the hospital. Fork left to leave the outward route at the next junction, taking the signposted 'High Weald Landscape Trail', pass the hospital entrance and, at a junction where a private road goes to Plummer Farm, look carefully for a well-waymarked footpath in the angle of the junction.

5. Follow this path between high hedges, then along the edge of a cultivated field to a waymark on a post, at a junction of two paths. Turn half left to continue across the field on a marked path, pass another waymark, then go over a stile to the next field, keeping close to a hedge on the left. Pass a little pond behind the hedge on the left, descending the side of the shallow valley to a waymarked stile. Go round to the right, as indicated by the waymark and cross another meadow, close to the hedge on the right. Cross a waymarked bridge, with a stile at each end, still following the Landscape Trail. Turn left, along the edge of a small, flat, meadow, crossing a similar waymarked bridge with stiles, to head for double gates, crossing the railway line over a level crossing.

6. Go over a waymarked stile on the far side of the track and cross a cultivated field, diagonally, as indicated, heading for a wind pump on the far side. Cross a watercourse on a concrete bridge and carry on along the right-hand edge of the next field to a waymark on a post. Turn right here, along a little path, through scrub and then along the edge of a field, taking the left-hand path at a waymarked junction. Cross a bridge over a watercourse and then traverse an enormous cultivated field, with unofficial marker posts defining the route, starting the ascent of the valley side. Reach a waymarked post at the far boundary hedge, crossing a plank bridge and then turning right to walk uphill on the far side of the hedge, towards farm buildings.

7. Pass through the attractive buildings of Lower Woolwich Farm, including a double oast, continuing along the access drive, still rising. Join a surfaced lane, turning left to Upper Woolwich Farm, another interesting collection of buildings. Turn right at a road junction opposite the farm and carry on to join a more important road on the outskirts of Rolvenden. Bear to the right to reach the lower end of the village, joining the main street beside the church. Turn right to return to your parking place.

11. Small Hythe

A circuit through fine countryside on rising land which, only 600 years ago, was close to the sea shore. The route rises steadily from its start at just above sea level to a summit at around 50 metres (164ft) but there are no steep gradients. Waymarking is good, as are the tracks and footpaths, with just the odd cultivated field to cross and a short section of overgrown lane. Roadside walking, at Small Hythe itself, is less than 1km (two-thirds of a mile). Twelve stiles.

Distance: 6km (3¾ miles).

Start/car parking: Substantial roadside layby at Small Hythe bridge, a short distance below the Ellen Terry house, grid reference 894299.

Maps: Ordnance Survey Explorer 125, Romney Marsh, 1:25,000. Ordnance Survey Landranger 189, Ashford and Romney Marsh, 1:50,000.

Tea Shop

Tenterden Vineyard, the home of Chapel Down wines, has extensive catering facilities. At first floor level, approached from the shop or preferably by the outside staircase, is a most pleasant terrace and the small tearoom. Here one can indulge in a Kentish cream tea or select from the cakes and scones displayed on the counter. More substantial food is available including salads, sandwiches, or plaited rolls with a choice of fillings. Hot meals served until 3pm. This café is particularly 'child friendly' with a 'drawing corner' and the children's special menu has a story on the reverse which will entertain them whilst waiting for the food to be served.

Open:10am to 5pm every day. Tel. 01580 763038.

Introduction

Only 600 years ago the now quiet roadside hamlet of Small Hythe was a busy little port, facing the Isle of Oxney across a wide arm of the estuary of the River Rother. The port served nearby Tenterden. In fact, Small Hythe was not only a port but also a place where small ships were built and launched.

There are a few fine old houses remaining in the hamlet, none finer than the 16th-century Small Hythe Place, occupied from 1899

Small Hythe Place

until her death in 1928 by the renowned actress Ellen Terry. Owned since 1939 by the National Trust, the house and its charming garden are open to the public during the normal National Trust season. Most of the house is furnished as it was during Ellen Terry's lifetime; the barn in the garden has been converted into an intimate theatre.

Just up the road, on the line of this walk, Tenterden Vineyard is one of the largest and best known in England, offering tours of the vineyard, wine tasting, shop, herb garden and spacious café.

Small Hythe church of St. John the Baptist, of the early 16th century, is built in brick, with stepped gables. The screen is original.

Nearby

The Isle of Oxney and the great flat expanse of Romney Marsh.

The Walk

Walk up the roadside, passing the National Trust-owned Small Hythe Place. Pass another lovely old half-timbered house and the unusual brick church, then the entrance to Tenterden Vineyard.

1. After passing a telephone box turn right into a waymarked foot-path, part of the High Weald Landscape Trail. Go through open gates and follow the marker down the right-hand edge of a large garden to a waymarked stile. Bear a little to the left to reach another waymarked stile. Cross a small field to a waymarked

gateway and bear right along the bottom edge of the next field to a stile, continuing to a plank bridge over a ditch and yet another stile. The next field may be cultivated; the route is indicated by a waymark, heading for the end of a hedge and a waymark on a post at the far side. Keep to the right of the hedge, go through a field gate and head for a stile. Dumbourne, with a fine double oast house, is passed, over a stile and a plank bridge. Go slightly left and then right to continue by a waymarked post, along the bottom edge of a cultivated field, with pheasants in abundance. Reach a waymarked stile and cross a field towards another stile. Do **not** go over, but bear left from the corner of the adjacent fence to commence a prolonged but not steep ascent, soon along a track heading for waymarked gates; below to the right is a large pond with waterfowl. Continue to rise to a stile beside locked gates and walk along a rough surfaced trackway, passing an impressive house, Ashenden. Stay with this drive, past a tiny pond, to reach the public road.

2. Turn left for a few metres, the turn right at a 'public footpath' sign, along a surfaced roadway past the side of a house. At the next property, Hongland, bear to the right, then pass Barnfield to reach a wide gate. Go through and carry on for 60 metres to a waymarked stile by a cluster of gates. Go along a grass path between fences to another stile then descend gently along a tree fringed sunken lane. Leave the wooded section to continue on somewhat overgrown grass, now level. Go straight across a farm track into another wooded area, pass a wooden clad house/smallholding and then another house set back to the left, as the track turns to the left.

3. In 100 metres, turn left again to leave the track by a plank bridge over a ditch and a stile. Follow the waymark pointing diagonally across the field, to a plank bridge and a waymarked stile, then a well-worn path over grass to another waymarked stile. Pass the end of a certificated caravan site and follow an agricultural track through the vineyard, bearing right and rising to reach the buildings. Bear right and then left to the tea shop. Leave the vineyard by its access roadway and turn right, along the roadside, to retrace the way to the car parking area.

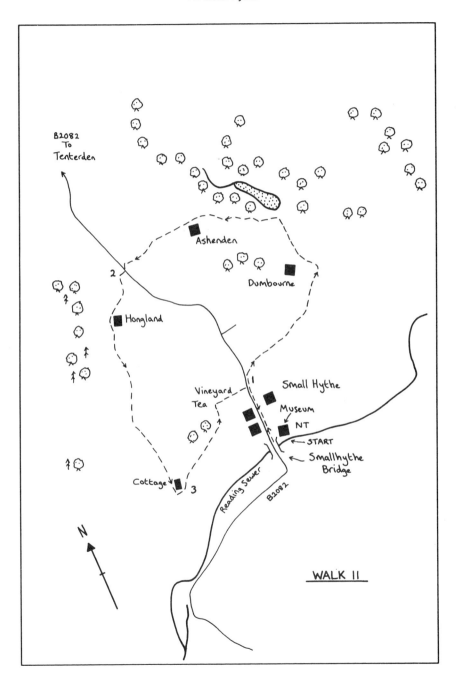

WALK II

12. Appledore and Warehorne

A little longer than most tea shop walks, this is a quite demanding circuit based on the well known village of Appledore, on the inland fringe of Romney Marsh. The outward route is through diverse agricultural land, with not all the sections of the path obvious on the ground. However, the waymarking is generally good and there are no serious ascents. The return route along the side of the Royal Military Canal could hardly be easier; no navigation required, completely level and a good grass path underfoot. Twenty-two stiles. Between them, the Saxon Shore Way and the Royal Military Canal Road (track) comprise the great majority of the walk. A shorter version, missing out Warehorne, is available.

Distance: 11.3km (7 miles). Shorter version 7.5km (4¾ miles).

Start/car parking: Behind the village hall, Main Street, Appledore, grid reference 956297.

Maps: Ordnance Survey Explorer 125, Romney Marsh, 1:25,000. Ordnance Survey Landranger, 1:50,000.

Tea Shop

Bayleaves is a delight – a really comfy tea shop. Seats and settles have lots of cushions; the tea rooms are adorned with photographs, dried flowers and grasses. There are baskets filled with a variety of bread which is baked on the premises and available to buy; the coffee beans were ground as we watched, producing a delightful aroma; the scones then came straight from the oven.

Morning coffee, lunches, and teas are served and afternoon tea is an enjoyable experience, especially following a fairly long walk. This is a tea shop not to be missed!

Open: Wednesday to Saturday 10am to 5pm; also open on Tuesday in the summer months. Tel. 01233 758208.

Introduction

Once a port and boat building centre on the estuary of the River Rother, Appledore has long been deserted by the sea, now several miles distant across the rich grazing land of Romney Marsh. The village stands a little more than 10 metres (33ft.) above sea level and the outward part of this walk reaches a height of about 30 metres. (98ft.). Despite these modest figures, the rise of the former sea shore above the line of the Royal Military Canal is a very noticeable landscape feature. The canal hugs the foot of the slope. Appledore straggles prettily along its only street, with Tudor houses, inns and shops. The 14th-century church is noted for its good glass.

At the far end of the walk, Warehorne is a tiny village with an inn and a 13th-century church showing an unusual combination of brick and stone in its construction.

The Royal Military Canal, more than 37km (23 miles) in length from Hythe to Rye, was built as a defence against Napoleon's threatened invasion. It was perceived that the flat lands and coast of Romney Marsh were particularly vulnerable. The north bank was protected by gun emplacements and signalling stations. Fortunately these defences were never put to the test. In World War II, the canal was again regarded as having defensive capability against Hitler's intended invasion and 'pill boxes' were built as reinforcements.

St. Mary's church, Kenardington, is plain but is high and light inside. The church may stand on the site of a Saxon fort.

Nearby

The fine old port and historic town of Rye is just over the county boundary in Sussex, a few miles to the south west of Appledore.

The Walk

From the car park turn left to walk along the roadside pavement, away from the village centre. Pass public conveniences and the recreation ground on the right. Turn right at the far end of the recreation ground along a minor surfaced roadway with a 'public footpath' sign. Go through a metal gate with a 'Saxon Shore Way' waymark and turn left at once to walk beside a ditch, with houses and gardens on the left. As the hedge on the left ends, go diagonally to the right, as indicated by a waymark on a post, crossing the field to a stile and plank bridge over a ditch. The path is now more obvious; Go over a stile and cross a cultivated field, heading uphill to a pronounced tumulus.

1. The right of way appears to go over the top of the tumulus; many walkers will no doubt prefer to skirt the foot. In a further 50 metres, at the edge of the field, go right to follow the Saxon Shore Way, keeping to the right of the line of trees. At the far end of this field, the Way bends a little to the left to continue along a narrow path. Do **not** turn fully left along a temptingly wide track. Aim for a gap in the hedge opposite, where there is a waymark on a post. Go across a large cultivated field; there is a marker post at the far boundary 20 metres to the left of a prominent clump of undergrowth. Cross a ditch on a plank bridge and follow the line indicated by the waymark across the next field to a marker post, 'public footpath' sign and stile at the top of the field. Cross a minor road at a 'footpath' sign, go over a plank bridge and up a few steps to reach another large rising cultivated field. Aim well to the right of a pair of isolated trees to a marker post, stile and a few steps down to a sunken lane. Go over a stile, up a few steps and then over another stile, all waymarked. In 40 metres go over another stile and carry on along the bottom edge of a field, with a fence/hedge on the right for about 100 metres, then go straight ahead across the field. If there is an obstructive crop without an established path, a better line here might be to stay close to the boundary on the right for some distance, gradually bearing to the left. As that boundary turns away to the right, an agricultural track across part of the field leads to a marker post and stile.

2. Go over the stile and join a minor surfaced lane. *Turn right here for the shorter version of the walk. The lane leads directly to the Royal Military Canal. Join the full route here, turning right to follow the canal side track back to Appledore.* To continue the full route turn left for 15 metres then turn right over a waymarked stile and go along the edge of a great meadow, with a hedge on the left, to head for St. Mary's church, Kenardington, situated well away from the village which it serves. Go over a stile into the churchyard. Turn right at once to head for a waymarked stile. Go over and head along the edge of a meadow to another stile, the path just visible on the ground. Go over a double stile and continue to a stile and plank bridge over a ditch and up to a footbridge over the Horsemarsh Sewer, nothing like as nasty as it sounds. Cross another footbridge and bear slightly left towards a marker post by a far hedge. Go over a stile and follow a clear path rising diagonally across a cultivated field to a waymark and stile at the top corner. Turn half right to carry on along a track across the next rising field, aiming roughly half way between a house on the left and a hedge on the right. Go over

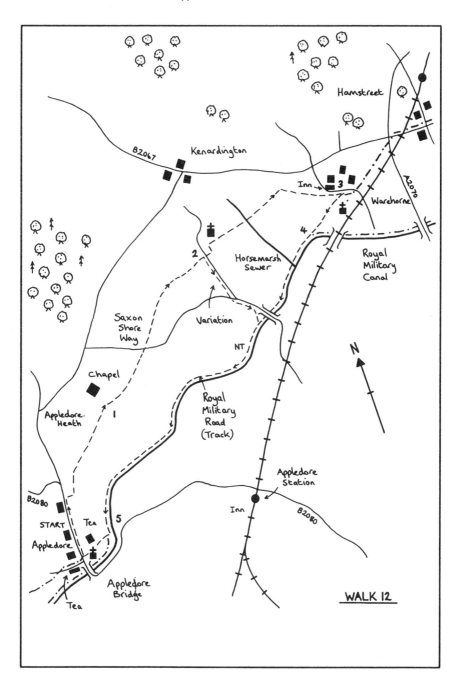

WALK 12

a stile and head for Warehorne church, through a farm gate, turning left to join the public road and then right to walk to the church and the inn.

The Woolpack Inn at Warehorne

3. Opposite the inn turn right, through a gate in front of the church and then immediately right again, over a stile. Cross part of the churchyard, leaving by a stile in the far right corner. Follow the line indicated by the waymark to cross a large, descending meadow, which might have temporary stiles over electric fences part way down. Bear right to join an agricultural track descending from the adjacent Tinton Manor Farm. At the bottom there is a wide, possibly muddy, gap, with a fence on the left and a hedge on the right. In about 25 metres look carefully for a waymarked stile and a little footbridge on the left.

4. Go over and turn right to walk back towards Appledore on the north bank of the canal, fine walking on grass. In a little more than 1km (three-quarters of a mile) the track, gated on either side, crosses the lane which is the connecting link for the shorter route. This bank of the canal is well-wooded, hawthorn and bramble being particularly prominent, and the whole of this length, owned by the National Trust, is noted for wildlife, particularly birds. The edge of Appledore village eventually comes into view; ignore a path on the right and pass farm buildings.

5. In 150 metres after the farm buildings turn right, over a plank bridge and a stile to follow a path, soon reaching a surfaced roadway and continuing to the village street. Turn right to reach the tea shop in 80 metres. After refreshments turn right to walk along the roadside pavement back to the car park.

13. Lydd

A short, level, undemanding, ramble through and around the little town of Lydd, just about enough to provide justification for a refreshment stop and give a tiny taste of the character of Romney Marsh.
Underfoot are stony driveways, grass footpaths, a little overgrown in places, and the public road through Lydd. One stile.

Distance: 3.3km (2 miles).

Start/car parking: Free car park by the Banks Sport Area, accessed along Dennes Lane, which leaves the main street opposite the church in Lydd, grid reference 040213.

Maps: Ordnance Survey Explorer 125, Romney Marsh, 1:25,000. Ordnance Survey Landranger 189, Ashford and Romney Marsh, 1:50,000.

Tea Shop

The Moon and Stars is not easy to find without directions. However, this pretty little café deserves a visit – the sign in the window welcomes you from wherever you come!

Beverages include tea, coffee, soft drinks, milk shakes; but a less usual choice might be Bovril served with a cream cracker. Savouries include 'sizzlers' of chicken, beef, or vegetarian; tuna and pasta bake, and other platters. Apple cake is served warm with fresh cream. Open for morning coffee, lunches, teas, and suppers, but note the limited opening hours.

Open: Tuesday to Saturday 9.30am to 3pm. Additionally on Thursday, Friday and Saturday from 6.30pm to 10pm. Closed all day Sunday and Monday. It may be preferable to check hours when planning your excursion. Tel. 01797 321052.

Introduction

A large tract of rich pastureland, formerly part of the sea bed, Romney Marsh has long been associated with sheep grazing. The average height above sea level is between 2 and 3 metres and, since Roman times, has been protected by sea walls, most notably that at Dymchurch – see walk 14. As might be expected in such a desolate and underpopulated area, factual stories concerning smuggling of wool in the 18th century have been built upon to produce romantic legends involving mysterious goings on, generally at night – shrouded figures, strange cries and the snorting and muffled hoof beats of unseen horses. In the 'Doctor Syn' series of novels, Russell Thorndike uses the Marsh as an evocative setting for his stories.

Lydd is an attractive little place, with individual shops occupying many of the stucco and brick buildings which line the street leading to the 13th-century church. The latter has the distinction of being the longest in Kent and is one of two apparent contenders (the other is nearby New Romney) for the title of 'Cathedral of the Marsh'. Side streets have distinctive weatherboarded houses and the overall impression is very favourable. It was once an important port, with 'Cinque Port' status, but tide and weather, particularly a great 13th-century storm, have left it stranded 5km (3 miles) inland.

Nearby

New Romney is another little town, again with good buildings, but with the disadvantage of having the main A259 as its High Street. There are inns, cafés, shops and a fine church. A little way out of town is the station and headquarters of the Romney, Hythe and Dymchurch Railway.

Old Lighthouse at Dungeness, open for visitors.

Dungeness Nuclear Power Station visitor centre and a nature reserve in the south-west tip of Kent.

The Walk

Leave the car park along a broad stony bridleway, heading towards gravel workings some distance ahead. Pass a flooded gravel pit on the right. As the track bends towards a dwelling, go straight on, through a waymarked gate, now on a public footpath. The path is narrow, between bramble, a little overgrown in places. Pass another flooded gravel pit; a fair amount of bird life, including flocks of geese, can usually be seen here. Carry on at a junction.

1. Turn left over a stile to join a wide track, heading for farm buildings. Pass a waymark on a post and go diagonally across a small field on a well-worn track to join a concrete access roadway. Bear left, over a redundant cattle grid, then cross a major drainage ditch. Pass Pigwell Farm, an apparent rest home/graveyard

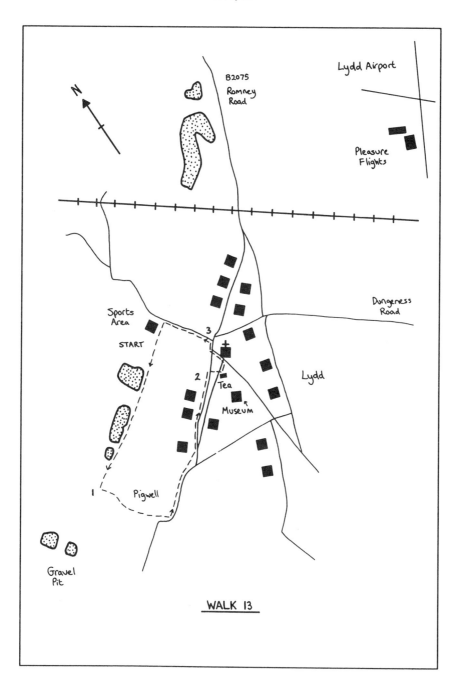

WALK 13

for old caravans, and join the public road. Turn left to walk by the roadside into Lydd. Pass the ornate boundary sign, then keep left for the town centre at a fork, to continue along High Street, heading towards the church tower at the far end.

Lydd parish church

2. Part way along the High Street, turn right, into New Lane, rich in lovely weatherboarded buildings. The Moon and Stars tea shop is in Park Street, opposite the end of New Lane. From the tea shop, turn right to walk past the public conveniences and reach a little square. Turn left here into Cannon Street, join High Street, and turn right. Turn left in a few metres into Dennes Lane.

3. Walk along the roadside pavement for about 300 metres before turning left at the 'public bridleway' and 'Banks Sports Area' signs to return to the car park.

14. Hythe and Dymchurch

A truly level linear walk across Romney Marsh, by no means as dull at that might imply. The Royal Military Canal path, the Romney, Hythe and Dymchurch Railway and the sea wall at Dymchurch all add variety, producing a good walk. Most of the paths are good although not always well-defined on the ground. With the exception of short distances on the fringe of Hythe and in Dymchurch, there is no roadside walking. Seven stiles. The recommended return to Hythe is by using the railway, a pleasant ride across the marsh. Alternatively, and particularly useful out of season, there is an hourly bus service along the A259 between Dymchurch and Hythe.

Distance: 9.5km (6 miles).

Start/car parking: Romney, Hythe and Dymchurch Railway car park, by the station, Hythe, grid reference154347. A modest charge is made.

Map: Ordnance Survey Explorer 138, Dover, Folkstone and Hythe, 1:25,000. Ordnance Survey Landranger 189, Ashford and Romney Marsh, 1:50,000.

Tea Shop

When almost giving up hope of refreshments in Dymchurch, one comes to the welcome Dr Syn's Restaurant and Tea Shop. The friendly proprietors welcome walkers; nothing is too much trouble and prices are reasonable. Open for morning coffee, light lunches, and afternoon teas. Cream teas are served and do try the truly home baked cakes including Victoria sponge and coffee and walnut cake. Bed and breakfast is available and evening meals by arrangement. Roast lunches served on Sundays – booking essential.

Open: Wednesday to Saturday 10am to 4.30pm all the year. Tel. 01303873159.

Introduction

Stretching beyond the line of the former sea shore which is marked by the scarp rising to the Lympne area, the great expanse of Romney Marsh, criss-crossed by drainage channels, is largely populated by fat contented sheep. There are a few winding little roads, a few paths, and even a few people, at places like Burmarsh. Out of season the feeling of remoteness is strong, particularly on a wild day. None of the marsh is significantly above sea level; over the centuries, from the Romans onwards, defensive sea walls have been constructed.

Hythe is an old town by the edge the Marsh, with a compact centre, alleyways and little streets rising to the great old 13th-century church. Of considerable importance was Hythe's status as one of the Confederation of Cinque Ports. The maritime connection is now limited to a seaside holiday area, separated from the town by The Royal Military Canal (see walk no. 12). There is no lack of shops, inns and other refreshments. The town has the eastern terminus of the renowned Romney, Hythe and Dymchurch Railway.

Dymchurch is an altogether smaller place, a historic village which has virtually disappeared under the trappings of a small seaside resort, with low key holiday facilities. The ancient 'capital of the marsh', Dymchurch has been protected since Roman times by a great sea wall, in its present form more than 6km (about 4 miles) in length. The church has three fine arches – the wide chancel arch and two Norman doorways.

The Romney, Hythe and Dymchurch Railway was built to 15-inch gauge in 1927 by Captain Jack Howey, using his great personal wealth to incorporate expensive features such as station buildings and double track, not normally found on miniature railways. At Hythe, the generous station is complimented by signal box, water tower, turntable, gift shop and café. The headquarters of the line at New Romney has similar facilities, plus toy and model museum, offices, works and sheds. The motive power is provided by scaled down versions of famous full size locomotives such as the 'Flying Scotsman' Pacifics which Sir Nigel Gresley built for the London and North Eastern Railway, and some North American designs. During World War II an armoured train was constructed. The line, across the marsh, is level. Daily services operate from April to September, with weekend only workings in March and October.

Nearby

The port and large town of Folkstone.

The visitor centre at Dungeness nuclear power station and the

The Romney, Hythe and Dimchurch Railway

nearby old lighthouse are a short distance from the western terminus of the Romney, Hythe and Dymchurch Railway.

On the scarp overlooking the Marsh are the castle and church at
Lympne and the well-known wild animal park at Port Lympne.

The Walk

From the car park, walk round the front of the station, pass the Light Railway Restaurant, then turn left at a 'public footpath' sign, along the side of the Royal Military Canal. Follow this path, squeezed between railway and canal, for about 1.5km (1 mile). Pass the end of a footbridge over the canal to continue for a further 300 metres, now with a road close on the left.

1. As the road bends away from the canal, turn left through a wide gap in the hedge to join the road beside an iron garden entrance gate. Carry on along the roadside pavement. As the road bends to the right, turn left at a 'public footpath' sign to pass a vehicular barrier and a children's play area. Cross a footbridge over a ditch and turn right, alongside the railway line. Go straight on over a waymarked stile. Cross a rough grazing area, keeping close to the ditch on the right, with extensive flooded gravel workings to the left; the scarp marking the former sea shore is now prominent to the right. Turn right, then left, at a waymarked concrete bridge over the ditch and carry on along a worn path across the middle of an extensive grazing area, to head for Botolph's Bridge. Pass to the left of sheep pens and a traditional shepherds' mobile hut, then bear to the right to a stile.

2. Join a public road, turn left, cross the bridge and pass the Botolph's Bridge Inn. Head along the road towards 'Aldington and Newchurch for 60 metres, then turn left at a signposted stile 'Romney Marsh Walk'. Bear a little to the right, over rough grass, to a yellow-topped marker post. Go diagonally across a field behind a works building, to reach a footbridge over a ditch. Continue across a great expanse of grazing land, heading for a waymarked stile. Go over and head for the near end of a fence, cross a ditch on a waymarked plank bridge, go over a stile on the left, and carry on with the fence on the right. Go through a field gate and cross over a wide watercourse at its junction with the main Willop Sewer.

3. There is a sewage works compound on the right as we bear left to cross the railway line, with a waymarked stile on each side of the track. Keep well to the right of Willop Sewer, crossing a meadow

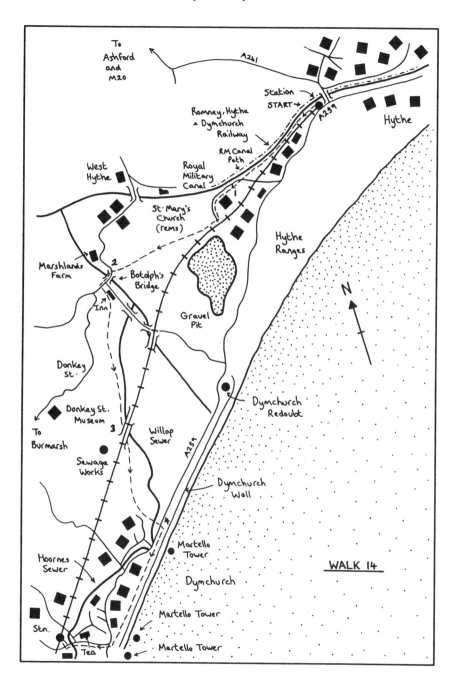

to a waymarked stile, then proceed across a huge cultivated area on a well-trodden straight line path. At the far end, reach a minor ditch, look carefully for a waymarked little footbridge, with a stile at its far end. After the stile, go to the left to head for a field gate flanked by yellow-topped posts. Pass through a small-holding, two more gates, and over a sleeper bridge across Willop Sewer. Fifty metres after the bridge turn right, then left, along a narrow path to the main A259 road. Cross over the road and go up a concrete ramp to the top of the sea wall. The extensive sea view includes the distant power stations at Dungeness.

4. Turn right, towards Dymchurch, walk along the sea wall for 2km (1$^1/_3$ miles), passing a Martello Tower on the way, to reach the beach area. Pass public conveniences then, opposite the boat-launching ramp, turn right to walk to the High Street. Turn left along the High Street and follow the sign towards the railway station. The tea shop is on the right in a short distance. From the tea shop, turn right, then bear to the left along Mill Road. Pass the fire station, cross Hoorne's Sewer, and turn right into Station Road to reach the railway station for the return to Hythe.

15. Lyminge

Quite a demanding circuit with a fair amount of rise and fall, involving parts of the Elham Valley Way, the North Downs Way and the Saxon Shore Way. The return is largely along the trackbed of the former Elham Valley railway line, with roadside walking through Etchinghill, Newington and Lyminge. Tracks are predominantly good, but with some crossing of cultivated fields. More than twenty stiles. Views, particularly from the downland section, are very good.

Distance: 10km (6¼ miles).

Start/car parking: Small free car park with public conveniences in Lyminge, opposite the parade of shops, grid reference 165410.

Maps: Ordnance Survey Explorer 138, Dover, Folkstone and Hythe, 1:25,000. Ordnance Survey Landranger 179, Canterbury and East Kent, 1:50,000 or Ordnance Survey Landranger 189, Ashford and Romney Marsh, 1:50,000.

Tea Shop

Lindsey's Larder in Lyminge is housed in premises previously used as a bakery. Lindsey has continued the tradition, baking and selling homemade bread whilst running the café. Furniture is of good solid pine and fresh flowers are on each table. The floor is 'boot friendly' and Lindsey welcomes walkers to this village tea shop. There is a choice of cakes, sandwiches, scones, as well as cooked meals including traditional breakfast. Roast lunches between 12 noon and 3pm on Sundays.

Open: 9am to 5.30pm except Wednesday when closure is 3pm and on Saturday at 5pm. This is a new venture and opening hours may be altered. You are welcome to check by telephone. Tel. 01303 862148.

Introduction

Lyminge is a large, sprawling, village, mainly modern, but with a few nice old buildings. Of greatest interest is the church, on the site of the original abbey church of St Ethelberga, who seems to have divided her time between this area and Northumbria. Some stones may be Saxon but most of the present structure is Norman. Inside the church, the massive 13th-century chancel arch and locally carved 20th-century oak pews are among the many features.

The village is situated quite close to the steeply sloping south face of the North Downs – Tolsford Hill, Summerhouse Hill, and the well-sculpted ends of the Downs behind Newington and is also close to the Channel Tunnel terminus near Folkstone. The railway line which connected Folkstone with Canterbury cut through these Downs, with a short summit tunnel at Etchinghall, then followed the Elham valley northwards. It has long been disused, with part of the trackbed now carrying the Elham Valley Way. There is a museum devoted to the history of the line at Peene, almost on the line of this walk.

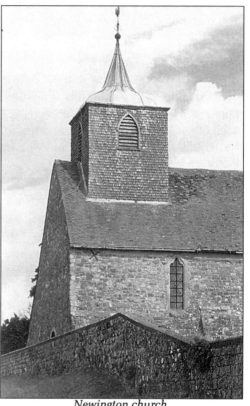

Etchinghall is a quiet little village with a pretty inn.

Newington and Frogholt are charming hamlets.

Nearby

Folkstone is close, a port for cross-channel ferries and a sizeable town with good shopping and other amenities.

Newington church

The Walk

Turn left from the car park, along the main street in Lyminge. Turn right, into Mayfield Road, then turn left at an 'Elham Valley Way' signpost into Rectory Lane. At the top of the lane cross the front garden of the Rectory to a gate/stile. Go over and along the top edge of a meadow to a waymarked stile, cross a paddock to another waymarked stile in 50 metres, then cross the public road to a stile opposite.

1. Follow the signposted footpath to the right, staying parallel with the road for 150 metres. Bear left to follow a line of mature trees, across a golf course. At the far end aim for a waymarked post ahead. Continue, with a hedge and ditch on the right, to another waymarked post in less than 100 metres. Bear left to go over a stile and join the public road. Cross over, bear left and go over a waymarked stile on the far side. Commence the long, steady, downland ascent along the edge of a field on a rather rough path, over another stile; the communications mast is dominant on the skyline ahead. Go over another waymarked stile and continue to rise up the middle of a huge cultivated field to reach another waymarked stile at the top boundary. The correct line across this field is to the left of the electricity pylon. Carry on over rough grass, passing a waymarked post on the way towards the communication masts. Go over a stile with several waymarks; follow 'Elham Valley Way', straight on.

2. On reaching the fence surrounding the compound, keep left, to a stile, and cross the access roadway to reach a fine array of waymarks. Go to the right, over a stile, and walk along the concrete track beside the compound to a waymarked post at the far end of the fence. Continue across rough grazing land on a discernible track, passing another waymarked post and admiring the fine downland views. Pass a trig. point on the left, then a tumulus on the right, to reach a waymarked field gate. Go through and follow a sunken lane, now descending the scarp. The track bears right to another field gate. Go through to carry on between outgrown hedges. At a waymarked cross paths turn left through a little gate to cross a cultivated field on a visible path, heading a little to the left of the distinctive Summerhouse Hill. Reach the top edge of woodland, then go through a little gate into the woodland. Emerge over a stile into a meadow. Cross the meadow, bearing a little to the right. Turn right at the end of the fence on the right, go through a field gate, then bear left at a waymark on a fence post, continuing with a fence on the right,

down a fine broad grass track; the M20 is now in view. Go over a waymarked stile, straight on with the fence close on the right. Go over a stile in the bottom corner and cross a cultivated field, heading for a waymarked post at the far boundary fence in 150 metres. Stay close to the fence on the right, go under a big oak tree, over a waymarked stile, then another stile in 10 metres.

3. Cross a minor road to a signpost and waymarked stile, then another stile. The narrow path weaves in and out across a patch of scrub, with large clumps of bramble, to reach a stile leading into the garden of a house. Go across, through a little gate, then down a few steps to a surfaced road. Turn left to walk past Froghall House and a thatched timber framed house of great antiquity, with a 'Kent Historic Building' plaque. As the road bends to the right, ignore a footpath on the left then, 10 metres further, turn left through a signposted small gate to follow what is, initially, an old sunken lane. Ignore any side paths; our track becomes a little overgrown before it reaches a barrier and the hamlet of Newington. Turn left at the quiet public road to walk through the hamlet, passing the village hall. Pass the Peene boundary sign and go through the dismantled former railway bridge; *the railway museum is a few metres further along the road.*

4. Turn left at once up a concrete surfaced track rising to a gate with an Elham Valley Way sign and join the former track bed of the railway. Stay with the former railway line for approximately 1km (two-thirds of a mile), rising at the gradient which took hard-puffing steam locomotives up to the tunnel at Etchinghall. As would be expected, the track is broad, permitting sociable, several abreast walking, with peeps at the shapely ends of the downland to the right. Continue through a waymarked field gate. Look out for a waymarked stile on the left opposite a private field gate on the right; despite the continuing attraction of the trackbed, you must leave the line here.

5. Go over the stile and turn right at once to follow a good path on grass above a cultivated field. Reach a patch of light woodland and carry on through a waymarked field gate. Another track

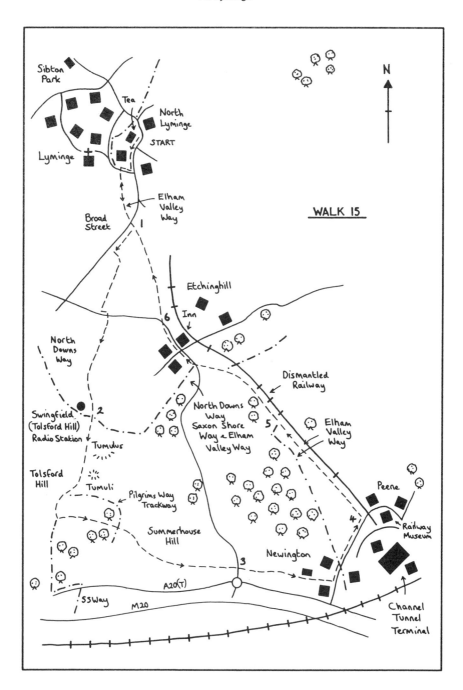

Sibton Park

Tea

North Lyminge

START

Lyminge

Elham Valley Way

Broad Street

WALK 15

N

Etchinghill

Inn

6

North Downs Way

Swingfield (Tolsford Hill) Radio Station

2

Tumulus

Tolsford Hill

Tumuli

Pilgrims Way Trackway

Summerhouse Hill

North Downs Way Saxon Shore Way & Elham Valley Way

Dismantled Railway

5

Elham Valley Way

Peene

Railway Museum

4

Newington

3

A20(T)

SSWay

M20

Channel Tunnel Terminal

joins from the right, under a former railway bridge. Bear left to a footbridge over a stream then, in 50 metres, go over a waymarked stile to rise up a steepish meadow, keeping to the right of a line of trees, to a stile right at the top, about 100 metres to the right of the prominent house. There is a great array of waymarks here, our route up the field is part of the North Downs Way. Join a minor road and turn right to rise to a junction with a more important road. Carry on into and through Etchinghill village, soon passing a motor depot and the village boundary sign. Pass the brick church, the corrugated iron village hall and the New Inn.

6. At the far end of the village, as the road bends to the left by the entrance to Etchinghill Golf Club, go straight on along a narrow path to a waymarked stile, join the golf club roadway, bear left before the clubhouse buildings, and then right to cross the course, following a line of white marker posts, a straight route on short grass. Rejoin the outward route at point 1, the roadside stile, to retrace that route across the paddock and back to the car park.

16. Elham Valley

A enjoyable country circuit based on Elham, a most attractive village in the valley of the same name. The Elham Valley Way is used for much of the route, combined with paths, a surfaced lane and a byway along the top of the valley side. Most of the tracks are very good, although there is a little rough ground. The ascent of the valley side is not really steep. Roadside walking is limited to half a km (a third of a mile) on a traffic-free country lane. Nineteen stiles.

Distance: 8.8km (5½ miles).

Start/car parking: Square by the church in Elham, grid reference 177439.

Maps: Ordnance Survey Explorer 138, Dover, Folkstone and Hythe, 1:25,000. Ordnance Survey Landranger 179, Canterbury and East Kent or Ordnance Survey Landranger 189, Ashford and Romney Marsh, 1:50,000.

Tea Shop

Parsonage Farm – the café at this visitor attraction is appropriately called 'the Shepherd's Hut'. The building is basic but well-suited to its environment and purpose. It is furnished with solid wood tables and chairs and interesting farming memorabilia is displayed. The menu too is appropriate for a farm visit and includes a ploughman's lunch, bacon and egg rolls, sandwiches, toasted muffins or crumpets, and cakes.

Open: 10.30am to 5pm every day from 1st April/Easter to the end of September. Closed on Mondays except for Bank Holidays. It may be advisable to check opening hours by telephone if in any doubt. Tel. 01303 840356.

Introduction

Gently pastoral, the Elham Valley must be one of the quietest areas in Kent, even the slight disturbance of the trains on the former railway line having long departed. The river is the Little Stour, more of an intermittent stream than a real river.

Once a market town, Elham was granted a charter in 1251 by the prince who became King Edward I. The Square is surrounded by the church of St Mary the Virgin, the ancient Kings Arms inn, timber and brick houses and tile-hung cottages. The flint and ragstone church, with origins in the 12th century, a tall spire and battlements, has been subsequently modernised, including the installation of windows depicting 19th-century figures such as Gladstone and Disraeli. There are more ancient buildings in the High Street, including the outstanding timber framed structure of 1614, now the Abbott's Fireside, used by the Duke of Wellington as his headquarters during the Napoleonic War. At the ends of the roof beams at the front are most unusual carotyd figures.

Parsonage Farm operates as a visitor attraction with rare breeds of farm animals, old farm machinery and the Shepherd's Hut tea room.

The Abbot's Fireside

The Walk

From the Square, walk down Duck Street, a surfaced lane with an 'Elham Valley Way' signpost. Pass the last house on the left, then turn left on a signposted footpath, along the bottom edge of a large field. Pass a field gate on the left then, in 60 metres, turn right where a waymarked post points the way, rising across the field an a good path, to commence the ascent of the valley side. Go over a waymarked stile, keeping the fence on the left to reach a waymark on a post at the top. Turn left here, to stay beside the fence, now rising more gently, with views back over Elham.

1. Reach a waymarked stile and go over, turn sharp right along the edge of a cultivated field then, in 30 metres, by the top corner of the fence, bear half left across the field on a well-defined path. Reach a fence by woodland and bear to the right to follow the fence as far as a waymarked stile on the left. Go over and along the edge of a cultivated field on a rough path. Go over a waymarked stile to join a very minor surfaced lane. Go almost straight across, then over another stile, cross the narrow end of a field to a signposted stile and join another minor lane. Go straight across to a stile with two waymarks, following that which points to the right, diagonally across a field, towards a farm building. Exit through a field gate to join a lane.

2. Turn left to pass Dreal's Farm then, in 70 metres, turn left through double farm gates at a public footpath sign. Walk along a short length of surfaced drive, passing the last of the buildings of the farm complex, then a silted pond on the left, to head for a field gate. Follow a well-trodden route diagonally across a big field, under power lines. Go over a waymarked and signposted stile to join a very minor surfaced road. Turn right, then left at a junction, to head for Wingate Farm. At a junction go straight across, keeping the farmhouse to the right, to a signposted 'byway', through double field gates and follow a broad green track running along the top of the valley side. Go through a field gate and continue, now with a hedge on the left, for 150 metres to another field gate. Go slightly downhill to join a farm track.

3. At this junction, there are waymarks on a post to the right. Take

care here, the relevant waymark is indistinct. Ignore the apparently welcoming gate 40 metres ahead; our route turns sharp left on a minor path across a field, to a waymarked stile in the hedge. Continue across a narrow cultivated field to a waymarked stile giving access to woodland. The steep descent through the wood needs care in wet weather. Go down a few rudimentary steps to leave the wood at a waymarked stile. Follow the obvious path diagonally across the field towards the farming hamlet of Wingmore. Go over/through a stile/gate and turn right, down a surfaced lane, to reach the valley road.

4. Turn left then, in 50 metres, turn left again at 'public footpath' and 'Elham Valley Way' signs to leave the road. Go over a waymarked stile on the right at once and angle across the field towards the far corner of a patch of woodland. Go over a waymarked stile at that corner to continue uphill, with a hedge on the right. Pass a waymark on a post; above to the left is Hall Down and the route is now noticeably on chalk. Another waymark on a post to the left shows the line to a waymarked stile at a cross fence. Carry on the same line; Elham is now in view. Pass another waymarked post; the path is now well-defined along the foot of the downland, with Parsonage Farm in view. Go straight on at a waymarked post; on approaching woodland, bear right, close to the hedge. Go over a waymarked stile in the far right corner and continue along a distinct path, passing a waymark, through an open gateway, and to a waymarked gate/stile. Go across a rough meadow, bearing a little to the right, to a waymarked gate, close to houses. Go ahead to a minor road. Turn right, crossing the trackbed of the former railway line, before reaching the right turn into Parsonage Farm, for the Shepherd's Hut tea room.

5. From the farm, go across the surfaced road, and follow a 'footpath' sign up a rising, broad, stony, track. Opposite the far end of farm buildings, turn left over a waymarked stile, then bear right to head for Elham, with a hedge on the right. Go over a waymarked stile at the near end of a line of poplar trees and continue along the edge of a field. Go over a waymarked stile on

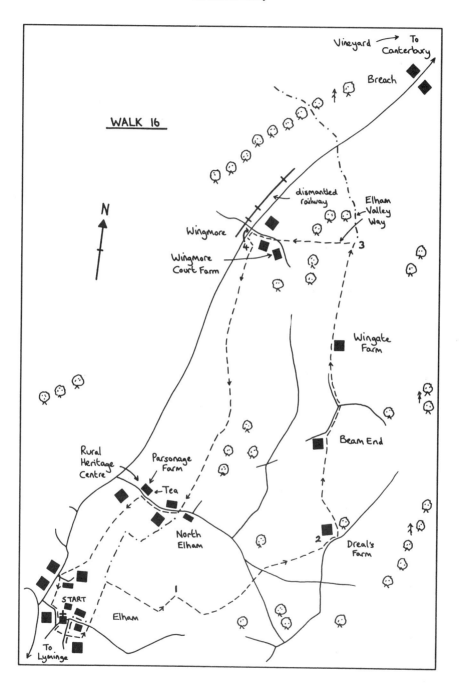

WALK 16

N

Vineyard → To Canterbury

Breach

dismantled railway

Elham Valley Way

Wingmore

Wingmore Court Farm

4

3

Wingate Farm

Beam End

Rural Heritage Centre

Parsonage Farm

Tea

North Elham

2

Dreal's Farm

START

Elham

To Lyminge

the right and follow a beautifully mown grass path to a gate/stile to enter the fringe of the village. Go right at a surfaced road, Cherry Gardens, and up to join the main street. Turn left to walk to the village centre, passing the large Methodist church of 1839. Pass the Rose and Crown to return down St. Mary's Road to the Square.

17. Dover

Totally unlike any other walk in the book, this route links the Western Heights above the town of Dover with the Eastern Heights on the far side. The sea front promenade provides the link in each direction. Much of the route is on hard surface. This is very much a walk for the marine enthusiast as there are great views from above of both the Western and Eastern Docks; likewise those who are intrigued by historic fortifications will find a great deal of interest in the Western Heights defensive complex. Although the linking section is totally flat, there are steep ascents, including many steps, at each end. Part of the Saxon Shore Way and the North Downs Way is included. No stiles.

Distance: 6.5km (4 miles).

Start/car parking: Small free car park, with picnic tables, well up the hillside overlooking the Western Docks. Accessed from the first roundabout on approaching Dover along the A20 from the Folkestone direction, left turn, signposted 'Western Heights', grid reference 314407.

Maps: Ordnance Survey Explorer 138, Dover, Folkestone and Hythe, 1:25,000. Ordnance Survey Landranger 179, Canterbury and East Kent, 1:50,000.

Tea Shop

The new National Trust Visitor Centre 'Gateway to the White Cliffs' is architecturally in sympathy with its natural surroundings. The café is gleaming and inviting with counter service offering a choice of food and beverages. Hot soup and well-filled sandwiches make a welcome lunch after a blustery walk on the White Cliffs, or afternoon tea can be very relaxed sitting on the long terrace with panoramic views of the Channel and the ships plying to and fro between England and France.

Open: 1st March to 31st October 10am to 5pm every day. 1st November to end of February. 11am to 4pm every day. Tel. 01304 202756.

Introduction

Quite apart from its great importance as a port, particularly with regard to cross-channel ferries, Dover is a substantial town with a great deal to offer. It does seem a pity that so many visitors must, of necessity, speed down Jubilee Way, straight into the Eastern Docks, and depart across the sea, seeing nothing of Dover itself.

Firstly, the history. Situated close to the first Roman landings, it is evident that Dover was quickly assessed as of strategic importance; the lighthouse building later incorporated within the Norman castle on its great rock high above the town is claimed to be the best preserved remaining Roman structure in Britain. Beside the lighthouse, St Mary's Church bears witness to the presence of Romans, Saxons and Normans on this outstanding site, the part of England separated from the continent only by the narrow Straits of Dover and such a critical factor in defence against any threatened invasion. The psychological importance of Dover and its white cliffs to homecoming British people is profound, particularly in times of war.

The castle, which was started by William the Conqueror and much enlarged by King Henry II, became a large and formidable medieval fortress. It was subjected to a siege by the French in 1216, which almost succeeded. It is now cared for by English Heritage as a major visitor attraction. In the town, the White Cliffs Experience and the adjacent Dover Museum offer a comprehensive exhibition of local history in a modern format. Close by are the Roman Painted House and the Old Town Gaol in the Town Hall, whilst a little way inland is the beautifully renovated Crabble Corn Mill, which has the stone ground flour for sale.

Less well known is the vast complex of tunnels in the Dover cliffs. Originally medieval, they were extensively and secretly used as a military headquarters throughout World War II. The earlier fortifications on the Western Heights, including the remarkable redoubt, are now provided with information boards. Entry to the Grand Shaft, by means of which large numbers of men could rapidly deploy from the much higher barracks area, is possible from close to sea level.

High on the East Cliff, much of a former prison area has been acquired by the National Trust and a modern visitor centre, the Gateway to the White Cliffs, has been constructed.

Nearby

St Margaret's at Cliffe – see walk18.

The track leading to Dover Castle

The Walk

Leave the car park by the minor path at one end, straight into St. Martin's Battery, a formidable defensive gun position, well explained by information boards, as are the other various fortifications in the area. At the far end go to the right, down steps to a footpath and then go down several consecutive flight of steps to a kissing gate. Go round to the left and then down a few more steps to another gate and a 'Grand Shaft' signpost. Continue along a surfaced roadway which bends sharply to the left to return across the hillside at a higher level. Leave this roadway at a complicated barrier and turn sharp right, back along a lesser roadway, entered through an open gate. In 60 metres turn left to go through a tunnel with a very constrained cross-section – rucksacks off here for large bodies! The tunnel leads to the sunken grass area which surrounds the mighty Drop Redoubt.

1. Turn right and go round the redoubt to a waymarked post. Turn right to leave the redoubt, descending towards the sea, fairly steep and slippery when wet; the luxuriant vegetation includes wild cabbage. At a junction, turn left, up a few steps, to a waymarked kissing gate. Turn right to continue the descent, helped by steps, down a grass bank; Dover Castle dominates the view. Reach another waymarked gate in 70 metres and carry on down a great flight of stone steps – care needed if greasy! Continue down a broad gravel track, to a Saxon Shore Way and North Downs Way signpost. Turn right to join Adrian Street, descending to a dual carriageway road. Go left to a pedestrian crossing. Cross and turn right to stay beside the road, bending left to find a pedestrian underpass.

2. Go under, turning right to reach the south east side of the main A20 road. Go straight ahead, past a war memorial, to the sea front, Marine Drive. Turn left to walk towards the Eastern Docks, less than 1km (two-thirds of a mile) distant. As the Marine Drive angles to join the A20, cross the A20 on a pedestrian crossing, bear right, then go along Atholl Terrace to follow a surfaced footpath rising above the vehicular entrance to the docks, towards Jubilee Way. The foot of the White Cliff is within touching distance on the left.

3. Pass under Jubilee Way and go up steps. Continue to rise on a surfaced path, soon reaching two parallel flights of steps. Keep to the right; the path continues to rise and there is a choice of route, including a path close to the edge of the cliff. Either route will eventually lead to the same place. Further inland, there is another, irregular, flight of steps leading to a 'public footpath' sign. Keep right here; for some distance the path is quite narrow, before reaching an open area, with telescope. Go down to the right here and then turn left to carry on along a fine terraced track with more views of the Eastern Docks.

4. At a junction of paths with seat and telescope, almost level with the end wall of the docks below, turn very sharp left on a surfaced path to reach the National Trust Gateway Visitor Centre for refreshments. *Should a longer walk be desired, a continuation from the above mentioned junction along the coastal path reaches the South Foreland Lighthouse in a further 3km (2 miles). This lighthouse is operated as a visitor attraction by the National Trust.* After refreshment start the return by walking down the visitor centre access drive to the footpath sign and

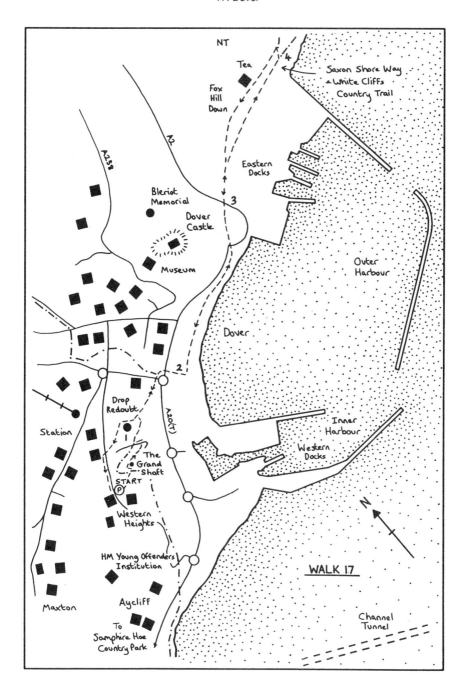

retrace the outward route along the Marine Drive. *To visit the town centre or any of its attractions, a right turn about half way along the drive is required. Do not be tempted to walk beside the busy A20 road.* Continue the return as far as the Drop Redoubt, via the underpass, Adrian Street and the great flight of steps. Go to the right to at the redoubt and around the far (north) side until a waymark on a post is reached. Leave the redoubt here, up steps and along a path between high walls, soon reaching a few more steps. Go through a waymarked kissing gate and down steps to another kissing gate. Turn left along the side of the public road, signposted 'St. Martin's Battery'. Continue over the top of the hill, pass the end of the road leading to the Young Offenders Institute and turn left into the car park in a few metres.

18. St. Margaret's at Cliffe

A very fine walk linking the inland village at St. Margaret's, the South Foreland lighthouse, the beach at St. Margaret's Bay and a unique tea shop, with a return through rolling agricultural countryside. The Pine Garden visitor attraction is also en route. Although the walk is not geographically long, in view of all the interesting features and a possible sojourn on the beach, not less than half a day should be allowed. Stony and grass paths are all first rate; there is a long ascent, up steps, from the beach. No stiles.

Distance: 6.5km (4 miles).

Start/car parking: Signposted small free public car park with public conveniences in village centre, grid reference 359448.

Maps: Ordnance Survey Explorer 138, Dover, Folkestone and Hythe, 1:25,000. Ordnance Survey Landranger 179, Canterbury and East Kent, 1:50,000.

Tea Shop

If a splendidly isolated situation on the cliff tops, immediately above the Saxon Shore Way, with views across the English Channel to France, appeals, then the Blue Bird could well be high on your list of favourite tea shops. Uniquely occupying a former coast guard lookout station, it has everything in its favour. Idyllic in summer and reassuringly cosy in winter, when gales are lashing the sea below and rain is battering against the windows.

On a more essential note, the menu is quite extensive, the usual range of tea, coffee, soft drinks, cakes and scones being supplemented from 12 noon to 2 pm by a range of hot snacks. Although quite small, the interior is walker-friendly, with a smart, practical, ambience. Open: All the year 10am to 5pm in summer and 10.30am to 4.30pm during the winter. Closed on Mondays (except for Bank Holidays) and Fridays. Tel. 01304 853520.

Introduction

S t. Margaret's at Cliffe is a high-lying substantial village with pleasant old buildings, some weatherboarded, several inns and essential shops. There is also a Norman church with a massive tower, two magnificent doorways and a well-decorated chancel arch. The beach at adjacent St. Margaret's Bay is reached by a winding little road tumbling steeply down the cliff to a small car park, beach café and public conveniences. Close to beach level is the Pines Garden, with specimen trees and shrubs, ponds and visitor facilities including shop and tea room, open during the season.

The cliffs are backed by an area of land owned by the National Trust which includes remnants of ancient grassland supporting an exceptionally rich flora including four kinds of orchid, ox-eye daisies and rock roses. Bird life and butterflies are similarly abundant.

South Foreland Lighthouse is owned by the National Trust and is open to the public during the season.

Nearby

Dover and the National Trust White Cliffs Gateway Centre – see walk 17.

Kingsdown, Walmer and Deal – see walk 19.

The Walk

Walk back to the village main street and turn right. Turn right again at once along Reach Road. In about 200 metres turn left at Reach Close; there is a 'public footpath' sign and a telephone box on the corner. Carry on to a large grass area at the heart of a residential estate and bear right. Go along the road on the right for 40 metres and then turn left along a concrete surfaced public footpath behind house gardens.

1. Cross a cultivated field on a well-marked diagonal path, to an opening in the far right corner. Take the left-hand of the two paths here, soon passing the gable of a bungalow before reaching a stony roadway. Turn right and continue on this roadway for about 500 metres, passing Briar Cottage on the way to a junction which has signposted footpaths to right and left. Turn left; South Foreland Lighthouse comes suddenly into view.

2. Join the Saxon Shore Way, to head for St. Margaret's Bay, turning left at a waymarked post. Follow a broad roadway, with sycamore woodland to the left, for 80 metres to a junction, where

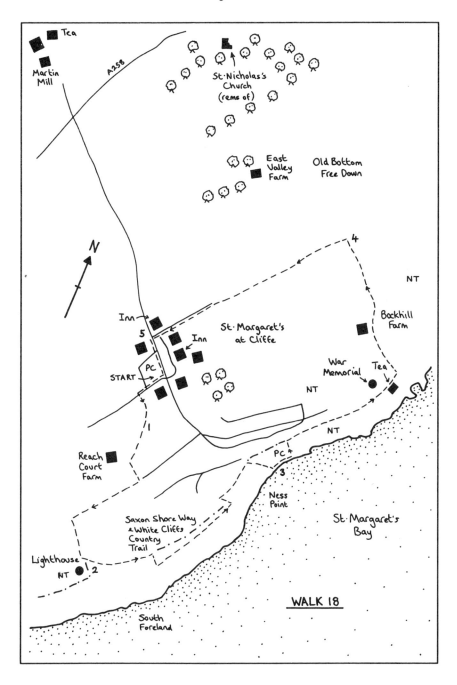

WALK 18

there is a waymarked post in the foliage to the left. Turn right here, with sudden views over the bay, the white cliffs and the Dover Patrol monument. The roadway becomes stony, with wild cabbage among the plentiful vegetation. Pass Cliff House then, just after the end of a high boundary fence, turn right, through a kissing gate, initially towards the sea. There are several path variations over the rough grass; that nearest the cliff top is waymarked; head generally towards the monument. Go downhill to a fence with an old 'path closed' board, turn left through a kissing gate, rejoin the more major track and descend to a junction in 150 metres. Turn right to walk downhill on a broad roadway, which soon becomes surfaced, passing St. Margaret's Museum and The Pines Garden. Continue along Beach Road, another road and then the road leading down from the village, to complete the descent to the beach.

3. Pass the tea shack and the public conveniences, then turn left at a signpost in a further 40 metres to start the demanding ascent of the cliff face by ingenious and seemingly interminable flights of steps. Turn right at the top, keep right at a fork and reach a kissing gate by a waymarked post and a National Trust sign. Go straight ahead, still rising, with the occasional waymark as encouragement. There are houses above to the left as the monument is approached. At a fork go either right or left; it does not really matter. If the right fork is taken, turn left up the slope before reaching a kissing gate through which the Saxon Shore Way continues. Turn right to visit the tea room. From the Blue Bird turn right, passing the field gate

At the Blue Bird Café

with a National Trust, 'Bockhill Farm' sign, to follow a broad grass track to a waymarked post in 50 metres. Turn left here, along a grass track between cultivated fields, soon with a hedge on the left. At a junction turn right, then bear to the left, now following a broad farm track dipping and then rising across St. Margaret's Free Down.

4. About 100 metres after topping the rise turn left at a junction to pass an old gate, where we leave the National Trust land. Proceed along a sunken track, soon joining a surfaced roadway signposted as a bicycle route. Stay with this roadway back to St. Margaret's village, passing the flintstone National School of 1849. Join the main street by the Red Lion Inn.

5. Turn left, passing shops, petrol filling station, phone box, the village sign, post office, Smugglers Inn and the Clyffe Inn before turning right to return to the car park.

19. Kingsdown

A circuit with plenty of variety, the Saxon Shore Way/White Cliffs Country Trail being linked with inland footpaths and bridleways, including a return over the National Trust owned Wood Hill. Three quarters of a kilometre (half a mile) along a minor road. Rise and fall are modest, with no difficulties whatsoever and no stiles.

Distance: 6.8km (4¼ miles).

Start/car parking: Informal back of beach parking place, in front of the Zetland Arms Inn. Approach – slowly! – along the private South Road, at the lower end of Kingswood, grid reference 380484.

Maps: Ordnance Survey Explorer 138, Dover, Folkstone and Hythe, 1:25,000. Ordnance Survey Landranger 179, Canterbury and East Kent, 1:50,000.

Tea Shop

The proprietor of Kitty's Tea Room is justifiably proud to have won the award made by Kent County Council in association with Kentish Fare for the best cream tea. The scones and cakes are certainly delicious and the toasted teacakes or sandwiches can be an addition or alternative to the traditional tea. Cooked meals available between 12 noon and 2pm and roast lunches are served on Sundays. Children are most welcome -high chairs available and a special menu too.

Open: Hours are somewhat restricted and could vary; if in any doubt do telephone first. Summer: Wednesday to Sunday and Bank Holiday Mondays, 10.30am to 5pm. Winter: Thursday to Sunday, 10.30am to 4.30pm. Closed all January. Tel. 01304 373755.

Introduction

Of no particular significance, but a quite attractive backwater, Kingsdown is barely 2km (1⅓ miles) south of the better-known Walmer. There are terraces of old houses reaching down to the sea, three inns, the occasional shop and a large holiday village. Formerly a port, Kingsdown had a lifeboat for many years. Inland, the North Downs roll towards the sea, with alternating hills and bottoms.

The beach at Kinsdown

Nearby

The ancient port of Deal now comprises an old (17th to 19th century) town clustered just inland from the sea front, a seaside holiday town with a great historic underlay, not least the remains of the castle built by King Henry VIII. The expected invasion by French and Spanish forces after Henry's break with Rome, which caused Henry to create powerful defences along the south coast, never material-ised. The damage to the castle occurred during the Civil War and by a German bomb in World War II. St. Leonard's Church is part Norman. Deal has museums and a part pedestrianised High Street with plentiful shopping and refreshment provision.

Adjacent Walmer is effectively a continuation of Deal, but with its own Henry VIII castle, owned by English Heritage, open to the public as a visitor attraction.

The Walk

From the Zetland Arms head north, towards Deal, along the coastal footpath, initially a tarmac track in front of a line of houses; the stony beach has quite an array of seaside vegetation, including sea kale. The track soon becomes a pebble-surfaced roadway, continuing

beyond the residential development as a surfaced footpath; the flag
visible above the trees ahead is at Walmer Castle.

1. Before reaching the flag, turn left at a post waymarked for
several local walks. Go along a narrow path, leading to a public
road in 50 metres. Go almost straight across to a 'public footpath'
sign, to rise along a good path beside the wall of Walmer Castle.
At the top of this path go straight across a narrow common,
Hawks Hill, then descend to the right to join a farm track for
about 50 metres, downhill to the public road. Turn left at the
road to walk along Rays Bottom for 0.8km (half a mile); there is a
former windmill in view across the field to the right.

2. As the gradient steepens, fork right, along a signposted public
bridleway, between hedges; this is Knights Bottom. At a crossing of tracks, with a post covered in waymarks, go straight on,
soon rising gently along the bottom edge of a large field. Go
through a gate, cross a minor road, and continue on a signposted
bridleway along Great Combe. The path enters a strip of woodland. Pass a post with a blue waymark on top then, in 40 metres,
rake back to the left to rise fairly steeply for a few metres, then
bear right to follow a fenced track along the edge of a field, with
woodland on the right. The National Trust owned Wood Hill is
directly ahead. Cross a farm access road and continue to rise,
along a waymarked footpath, up the left-hand edge of a field.
Enter the woodland through a green arch and keep to the track
which initially bears right, near the fringe of the wood, before
bearing left to carry on round to the exit point, passing a chalky
area on the way. The exit point is at the far end of the
diamond-shaped wood which covers the top of the hill. The
path now keeps close to a hedge on the left, with a brief glimpse
of the sea, to reach a barrier and a junction of paths.

3. Turn left, then go straight on at the next junction in a few metres,
soon passing along the backs of high fenced back gardens,
before descending to join the public road. *For the shortest route
to the tea shop, do not turn immediately right, but cross the first
road and then bear right, downhill, through the main part of
Kingsdown village. At the junction at the bottom, go left to reach*

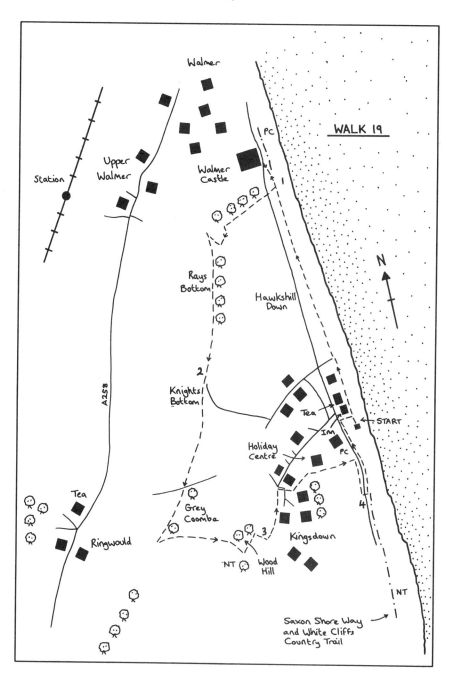

the tea shop in a few metres. For a more interesting return, avoiding the village road, turn right, into The Avenue, going left as the road forks to reach a 'public footpath' signpost at the end. Follow the path which turns right immediately, to descend between a scout camp site and a holiday village. At the bottom bear round to the right until a flight of steps on the left is reached.

4. Go down the steps and join a minor road, turning left to walk by the sea shore, passing public conveniences before reaching the road junction and the tea shop, as above. This route is about 0.7km (half a mile) longer than the more direct route. In either case walk back a few metres from the tea shop and turn left down North Road or South Road to return to the parking area.

20. Sandwich

An enjoyable level circuit linking the lovely little town of Sandwich with the nearby coast, crossing two golf courses on the way. Parts of the Stour Valley Walk, Saxon Shore Way and the White Cliffs Country Trail are incorporated. Underfoot, the surfaces are so good that the wearing of boots is not essential. Three stiles.

Distance: 6.5km (4 miles).

Start/car parking: Free public car park with public conveniences on The Quay at Sandwich, grid reference 333582.

Maps: Ordnance Survey Explorer 150, Canterbury and the Isle of Thanet, 1:25,000. Ordnance Survey Landranger 179, Canterbury and East Kent, 1:50,000.

Tea Shop

Sandwich offers a choice of tea shops; we chose the popular 'Friendly Little Cottage Tea Rooms' situated opposite the quay and enjoyed a lovely afternoon tea with very friendly service indeed. Tea of various blends is available, good quality coffee is served with refills offered at frequent intervals; the scones were warm from the oven. Cakes and toasted tea cakes are also tempting with afternoon tea. Cooked meals include tasty egg and chips or fish and chips.

Open: Summer months – Tuesday to Saturday, 9.30am to 5pm, Sunday 9.30am to 4pm. Winter months – Tuesday to Saturday, 9.30am to 3pm and Sunday 9.30 to 4pm. Tel. 01304 6143877.

Introduction

Founded by the Saxons and oldest of the Cinque Ports, Sandwich has a long maritime history. However, silting of the River Stour from the 16th century onwards now limits activity to nothing bigger than modest pleasure boats, which mingle attractively at the moorings with Thames style barges and the odd house boat. The sea is now the best part of 3km (2 miles) distant. The river does still form a defined edge to the town proper, fronted by the remains of the medieval barbican and the 13th-century Fisher Gate, the last remaining gateway through the town walls, parts of which still survive. The town centre is compacted behind the former wall, with fine old

The River Stour at Sandwich

buildings, some showing the influence of the influx of Flemish immigrants, mainly weavers, fleeing from religious persecution in the late 16th century. St Clement's parish church has a Norman tower of about AD1100. The other two churches, St. Mary's and St. Peter's can also claim Norman origins. In the late 16th century the latter was given to the Flemish and French immigrants. The tower collapsed in 1661, the replacement being provided with a bulbous cupola, more characteristic of churches in the Netherlands. The Guildhall, built in 1579, has been enlarged and modified in more recent times. It now houses the local museum. Also of great interest is St Bartholemew's Hospital, founded in 1190 as a resting place for travellers. The buildings form a square with the chapel of St. Bartholemew in the middle. There is still a community of 'brothers and sisters'.

Over its centuries as a port, the town saw the coming and going of monarchs and was several times attacked by sea-borne raiders. From the 17th century it has settled for a role as a peaceful market town (Thursday is market day), now with a considerable overlay of visitors. Inns, restaurants and shops are plentiful. The White Mill, of 1760, is claimed to be the oldest restored windmill in Kent, complete with original machinery. It is open to visitors. Two golf courses occupy the land which now separates the town from the sea. The beach is of shingle and sand, not exciting, but with good views across Pegwell Bay to Ramsgate. Boat trips on the River Stour are a considerable visitor attraction.

Nearby

The extensive ruins of the former Roman port, military and naval base, of Richborough are very close to Sandwich. Richborough was the main port of entry to Roman Britain.

Ramsgate, a fair-sized town, ferry port and resort is a few miles along the coast.

Deal and Walmer – see walk 19 – lie along the coast in the other direction.

The Walk

With the River Stour on the left, leave The Quay car park, passing a signpost for the Stour Valley Walk, to walk along a surfaced track, with a line of lovely willows to the left. Turn left over a footbridge to cross a tributary of the Stour, the Vigo Sprong. Carry on along a surfaced track, passing a waymarked post.

1. Go left at a post with Stour Valley Walk waymarks; the path is still surfaced, now on a low causeway staying fairly close to the river. Cross a tributary – The New Cut – pass a building on the

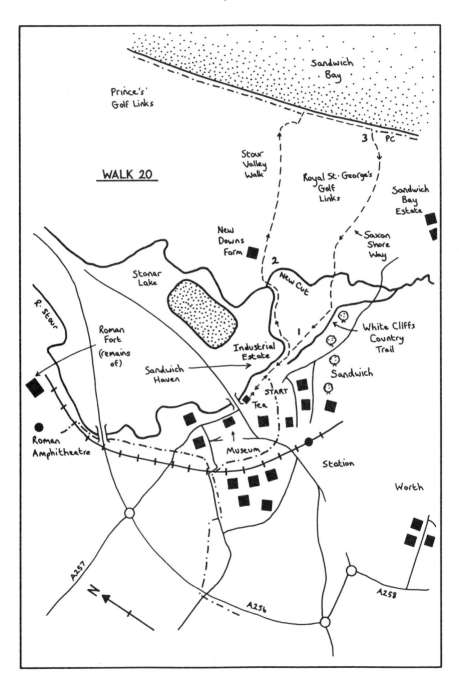

WALK 20

Sandwich Bay

Prince's Golf Links

Stour Valley Walk

Royal St·George's Golf Links

Sandwich Bay Estate

New Downs Farm

Saxon Shore Way

Stonar Lake

New Cut

R. Stour

Roman Fort (remains of)

Sandwich Haven

Industrial Estate

White Cliffs Country Trail

Sandwich

Roman Amphitheatre

START
Tea

Museum

Station

Worth

A257

N

A256

A258

right, and go through a waymarked gate to join a very minor road.

2. Turn left for 15m, then turn right, over a waymarked stile, to follow a well-worn path over rough grassland, passing a house to the left; in view ahead is a former golf clubhouse. Ignore a waymarked stile on the left to continue along a well-used path. Pass a waymark on a tall post, then go through a small, waymarked, gate and straight across a close mown area of golf course, to an unsurfaced roadway. Carry on past the redundant buildings to reach the coast. Turn right, through/over a gate/stile on a surfaced roadway to pass an informal car parking area; the beach is readily accessed here. *A local nature reserve has a blend, unique for south east England, of mud flats, salt marsh, sand dunes, cliffs and pasture, with Sandwich terns, oyster catchers, ringed plovers, painted lady butterflies, sea holly and marsh orchids.* Follow either the roadway or a parallel track to the left. In almost 0.8km (less than half a mile), opposite public conveniences, turn right, over a signposted and waymarked stile.

3. Follow the well-marked route across St. George's Golf Course, a little up and down as it weaves its way attractively through some of the rougher parts of the course. Leave the course at a kissing gate with a Saxon Shore Way waymark. Cross a minor road, passing 'footpath' signs and a redundant stile, cross the New Cut on a footbridge and follow a surfaced path to its junction with the outward route at point 1. Bear left to return to the car park and the tea shop.

21. Reculver

A level, easy, walk on tracks which are easy to follow and so good underfoot that the wearing of boots is hardly necessary. Part of the route is along the North Sea Wall and part along an embankment by the railway line, with a return along the Rushbourne Sea Wall. The whole route is close to the sea; the great gaunt towers of the ruin of Reculver church are never out of sight. Designated footpaths involved are the Wantsum Walk and the Thanet Coastal Path. No stiles.

Distance: 6.8km (4¼ miles). *A shorter walk of 4km (2½ miles) is available.*

Start/car parking: Large free car park with information centre and public conveniences by the beach at Reculver, grid reference 226693.

Maps: Ordnance Survey Explorer 150, Canterbury and the Isle of Thanet, 1:25,000. Ordnance Survey Landranger 179, Canterbury and East Kent, 1:50,000.

Tea Shop

On the basis of 'first find the tea shop' Reculver almost failed the test for inclusion in this book. However, the walk is good and the area is full of botanical, historical, and geological interest, so a compromise has been made. Certainly a typical tea shop does not exist in Reculver but for refreshments such as coffee, chocolate, crisps, chips and cooked meals try 'The Dive In' café in a parade of holiday entertainment premises, opposite the large car park. Alternatively the village inn – 'The King Ethelberg' – offers the usual range of pub food and all-the-year availability.

Introduction

On the north shore of the Isle of Thanet, Reculver is situated where a broad wedge of countryside meets the sea, unique in this area of seemingly endless coastal conurbation – Whitstable, Herne Bay, Birchington, Westgate, Margate, Broadstairs and Ramsgate. It is a small place with a remarkable history – Roman, Saxon, Norman and more recent. The remains of the Roman fort of Regulbium have, in turn, supported a Saxon monastery and a Norman church. Of the fort, about one third has since been taken by the sea, whilst the

Ruined church at Reculver

monastery was destroyed by the Vikings. Even the Norman church succumbed early in the 19th century, when the then vicar became fixated on the possible subsidence of the building into the sea and persuaded the parochial council, on a 4 – 3 vote, to agree to its demolition and replacement further inland. Perhaps fortunately, in view of their importance as a landmark for shipping, the Admiralty requested that the towers be left standing. Later in that century, for some time they carried Trinity House beacons.

Until the Middle Ages, Thanet really was an island; a wide navigable channel separated Reculver, on the mainland, from the nearby St. Nicholas at Wade, on the island. The channel has since progressively reduced to today's narrow ditch. Despite the modern accretions such as the large car park, the inn, the lobster farm, the intrusive caravan park and its shanty-like appurtenances, the feel of remoteness, even of mystery, which is peculiar to large areas of flat coastal marsh, has not entirely deserted Reculver and its surroundings, particularly on a desolate winter day.

As might be expected, the vegetation is an interesting mixture of salt marsh plants by the back of the shingle beach and freshwater marsh plants a few yards further inland. Some, such as the sea pea, are quite rare. Other plants include ragwort, sea holly, yellow horned poppy and common reed. There is also a good selection of coastal birds.

Nearby

The long established seaside towns of Whitstable, Herne Bay and Margate.

The Walk

Start in the direction of the ruined church, rising – the only ascent in the circuit – with the King Ethelbert Inn on the right. Pass the ruins and descend to the end of the caravan site. Turn left towards the sea at a signpost, passing part of the wall, including the east gate, of the Roman fort. Turn right, along the wide concrete track on the top of the Northern Sea Wall. Follow this track for 2.5km (1½ miles). For some distance, to the right of the route is a lobster farm.

For a shorter version of the walk, turn right in just over half this distance to follow an unsignposted grass-topped embankment which joins the return route on the Rushbourne Sea Wall.

Along the Northern Sea Wall, the differential vegetation is well seen on either side of the track. Ahead, Birchington and part of Margate can be seen. As the track bears a little way inland, the hollow to the left is filled by a salt-water lagoon.

1. Turn right, beside a 'Cold Harbour' interpretation board, to head inland to the railway line. The track is now unsurfaced but is still broad and easy, between drained and cultivated fields, with

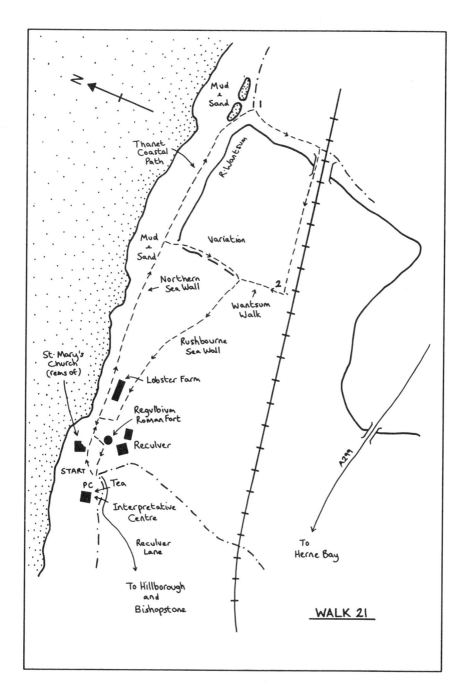

WALK 21

the River Wantsum on the right. On reaching the railway line and a junction of tracks, turn right, angling up to the broad embankment above the railway tracks. The altitude, just a few metres, enhances the views. Continue on comfortable grass, passing a post with waymark close to a foot crossing of the railway.

2. At the next junction, with a waymarked post and a railway crossing to the left, turn right, along the top of another good embankment, the Rushbourne Sea Wall. As the embankment bends to the left, there is waymark on a post. In a further 100 metres, go left at a waymarked post, to head straight for the great towers. *The short walk joins us here.* After passing the lobster farm, go to the right to a field gate and rejoin the outward route. Turn left to pass the church ruins and return to the car park. By staying beside the Roman walls, the rise over the church mound can be avoided.

22. Faversham and the creek

A straightforward level walk starting and finishing in the old town of Faversham, using the Saxon Shore Way and the Swale Heritage Trail to form a circuit inside the Faversham Creek and the Oare Creek waterways, around the perimeter of Ham Marshes. Most of the route is on a grass embankment. A little more than 1km (two-thirds of a mile) is on roadside pavement and town streets. Extensive boat moorings on the two creeks add interest to the circuit. Five stiles.

Distance: 8.5km (5¼ miles).

Start and car parking Any town centre car park in Faversham. The pay and display central car park, by the swimming pool, is easy to access from the signposted route leading from the edge of town A2 main road to the town centre and is, therefore, recommended. Grid reference 016613. The start and finish of the walk at the Market Place is about 100 metres from this car park.

Maps: Ordnance Survey Explorer 149, Sittingbourne and Faversham, 1:25,000. Ordnance Survey Landranger 178, Thames Estuary, Rochester and Southend on Sea, 1:50,000.

Tea Shop

At the heart of Faversham, in the Market Place, is the unmissable Shelleys Tea Shop. Tables and chairs are out on the pavement on sunny days whilst indoors is beamed, carpeted, calm and peaceful – a thoroughly relaxing atmosphere. Good quality coffees and teas of numerous varieties are served with scones or cakes – the individual treacle and Bakewell tarts are superb. Hot and cold dishes are available for lunch. On Sundays, when roast lunches are served, advance booking is advisable. Friendly service and reasonable prices.

Open: 9am to 5pm, Monday to Saturday; 11am to 4pm on Sunday. Tel. 01795 531570.

Introduction

A fine small town and port at the head of a long creek, Faversham is bounded by an apple-filled countryside. Granted its first charter in AD811, the town has the Market Place as its core, with historic buildings radiating in all directions. In 1147, King Stephen founded

Along the creek at Faversham

an abbey in Faversham. It was destroyed at the Reformation, but in Abbey Street the mellow brick and half-timbered houses have been progressively restored since the early sixties. Part of the abbey gatehouse was rebuilt into a house in 1538-40 by Thomas Arden, then Mayor of the town. He was murdered at the house in 1550; his tale is told in the well known play of 1552 – Arden of Faversham. Other old buildings include 17th-century warehouses on Standard Quay; materials from the ruined abbey were used in their construction. There is a great deal of the 14th century in Faversham's spacious church but the interior, although full of interesting features such as Norman windows and doorway, wonderful carved choir stalls, the unique Treasury and a rich and varied collection of brasses, has been heavily criticised for the destruction of the Norman nave and the erection of many extra pillars. The fine lattice work spire is comparatively modern.

In recent years the town has become a centre of the brewing industry and of fruit packaging, catering for the many adjacent orchards. Today, Faversham has excellent shopping, with abundant inns and restaurants, a small commercial quay and plenty of pleasure boating, tourist information office and the Fleur de Lis Heritage Centre housed in a former 16th-century inn building in Preston Street, displaying a thousand years of local history.

Just a few centuries ago, Ham Marshes were under the sea. They are now used as grazing land, with extensive gravel working and with boatyards fringing the two creeks which all but enclose the former marshland.

Nearby
Oare village gives its name to the tributary creek.

The Walk
From the central car park, walk for 100 metres or so to the Market Place, passing public conveniences, then go through a passage along the side of the NatWest bank. From the Market Place go straight ahead, heading north, along a broad street of elegant buildings, initially pedestrianised. Turn left at Quay Lane, bearing round to the left. Opposite the Shepherd Neame Brewery, turn right at a signpost 'Saxon Shore Way' and 'Swale Heritage Trail', into Bridge Road.

1. Cross the creek on the pivoting road bridge and turn right, at once, to follow the Saxon Shore Way across the front of a row of cottages, Front Brents. According to a nearby information board, Faversham was the 'King's Port', busy until the time of World War II. Pleasure boating is now obviously dominant. Pass the Albion Inn and continue along the waymarked, fenced path at the end of the terrace. Go round a development of modern houses then, at the far end, bend to the left to go round the inland perimeter of an industrial estate. Turn right at the far end of this estate to walk back to the creek, over a waymarked stile. Turn left at a waymarked post by the side of the creek to follow an excellent grass path, slightly raised on an embankment, with boats, ancient and modern, in profusion. Go over a waymarked stile, heading towards Nagden Cottages, passing a lagoon rich in waterfowl, with swans and coots prominent. Go over a

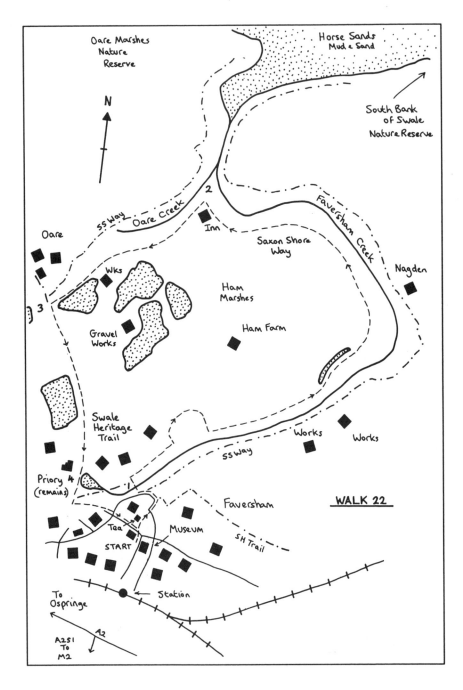

waymarked stile and continue, noting an immediate and dramatic change in the path-side vegetation. Go over three more stiles as you head for the Shipwrights Arms Inn, a pleasant, weatherboarded structure, reached through a little gate.

2. Pass the inn and turn left, to a waymarked post. Go straight on, following the Saxon Shore Way, soon on a low embankment beside Oare Creek, again with a great deal of maritime activity. Hawthorn and other small trees provide the first (and only) woodland of the walk. Join a surfaced roadway and turn right, soon on a road causeway between Oare Creek and flooded gravel workings.

3. Reach a public road and turn left along the roadside pavement, now following the Swale Heritage Trail, to pass an industrial estate, then a former windmill, close on the left. Pass the Windmill Inn and carry on to the site of the former Priory (the abbey founded by King Stephen). There is a Swale Heritage Trail sign on the opposite side of the road. Go ahead to descend Darrington Hill to a road junction.

4. Bear left to pass an attractive pond/recreation area, with many waterfowl. Go along Curtis Way, keeping left by the Bull Inn, to walk up West Street, lined by lovely, well-restored, old properties. Cross North Lane and continue along West Street, now pedestrianised and very much part of the town centre shopping area. Shelley's tea shop is on the left as the Market Place is reached. Retrace from the Market Place to the car park.

23. Brogdale and Painter's Forstal

An unassuming little walk, based on the National Apple Centre at Brogdale Farm. Some of the route is through apple country, using a variety of, mostly good, paths, tracks and the sides of minor roads. Two sections of footpath were found to be overgrown when checked and one small cultivated field is crossed. Modest amount of rise and fall, with a steep little ascent approaching Painter's Forstal. Three stiles.

Distance: 5km (3 miles).

Start/car parking: Large **customer** car park at Brogdale Farm, readily accessed from the main A2 road at Faversham, grid reference 006597.

Maps: Ordnance Survey Explorer 149, Sittingbourne and Faversham, 1:25,000. Ordnance Survey Landranger 178, Thames Estuary, Rochester, Southend on Sea, 1:50,000.

Tea Shop

Brogdale is one of the more unusual venues in this book. 'Pippins' continues the theme of fruit – especially apples – the menu cards have an attractive illustration of apples and the table covers are an apple design. Continuing the theme, drinks include apple juice or cider, the 'ploughman's lunch' provides the 'apple-a-day' and one of the savoury dishes is sausage and apple pie served with salad. There is a good choice of cakes including, inevitably, apple cake. Scones or the set cream tea may be tempting in the afternoon. Hot meals served between noon and 2.30pm are listed on the blackboard.

Open: Daily 10.30am to 5pm except in the months of January, February and March when it is open from 10.30am to 4.30pm but closed on Monday and Tuesday. Tel. 01795 535286.

Introduction

This walk is in genuine Kent orchard country, with the apple supreme. Brogdale Farm is home to the National Fruit Collections, with, believe it or not, over 2300 different varieties of apple, 550 of pear, 350 of plum, 220 of cherry and 320 varieties of bush fruit. The farm is also a considerable visitor attraction, with orchard tours, sale of fruit and plants, gift shop sales, a miniature railway and the Orchard Tea Rooms. Throughout the year there are special events, such as the Summer Fruit Festival in July and the Cider and Perry Festival in September.

Orchard near Brogdale

Painter's Forstal is a pleasant but unremarkable little village, with the Alma Inn.

Nearby

Faversham – see walk 22.

The Walk

From Brogdale car park, go back to the public road and turn left to walk along the roadside pavement. At the far end of a row of set back houses, and before a large former oast house, turn left along a narrow footpath, soon squeezed between trees and a boarded fence, with overabundant bramble and nettle growth. Part of the Brogdale orchards is visible to the left. Go through a kissing gate and down to a minor road. Cross over to the stile opposite and cross a narrow cultivated field, rising a little to the left to reach an opening into an orchard. Continue over grass along the edge of the orchard, with a tall hedge on the left.

1. Join a surfaced lane and carry on, passing Plumford on the left before taking a right fork, with a concrete 'public footpath' sign. Follow this agricultural track to Square Wood, on the right, with a large cultivated field to the left. The grass path goes on along the fringe of the next wood, now on our left. At the end of the field, dip to the left, into woodland, reaching a junction in a few metres. Turn sharp right, along a wide woodland track. At a fork in approximately 300 metres, go to the right, slightly uphill. At the next junction turn right, uphill. Follow this track through a pheasant-rearing area, still within a comparatively narrow belt of woodland with a great deal of beech. Leave the woodland at the edge of a large field, part cultivated. Turn right for 40 metres to a hedge, with an orchard beyond. Turn left to walk along the near side of the hedge on good grass. Join an agricultural track at the far end of the hedge. Turn left, downhill; Painter's Forstal village is in view on top of the low hill opposite. Towards the bottom, as the track bears to the left, look out for a little path, barely visible, which descends to the right, towards a tree-lined boundary about 40 metres distant. Turn right, to walk beside the boundary for a short distance. At the corner, go diagonally left to continue the descent towards houses which have been prominent for some time.

2. Bear left to cross a causeway over a ditch and pass between houses to join a minor public road. Turn left along the road. About 60 metres after passing the last house, turn right, into a narrow path with a concrete sign and rise sharply up the wooded hillside, aided by a few steps. The path is good initially, but there is some overgrowth by the side of a garden fence as Painter's Forstal is approached. Reach the village by the side of a former Wesleyan Chapel, now the Champion Hall. Cross the road and follow the roadside pavement opposite, towards Ospringe. Pass the trim Alma Inn and stay with the same road past a junction.

3. At the far end of the village, immediately before the entrance to Lorendon Preparatory School, turn right, over a stile, to take a narrow grass path between fences. By a large horse-chestnut tree the path forks. Go straight on, soon along a lovely grass path (part of the comprehensive work carried out by Lorendon Estate on this natural and very pleasant area of land), descending gently. Cross a ditch on a substantial brick bridge and join the public, road over a stile, at Whitehill.

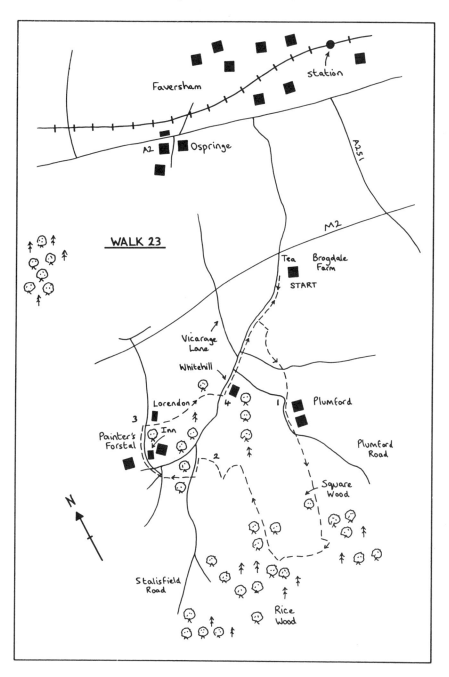

WALK 23

Faversham

station

A2   Ospringe

A251

M2

Tea   Brogdale Farm
START

Vicarage Lane

Whitehill

Lorendon

4   1   Plumford

3

Painter's Forstal   Inn

Plumford Road

2

Square Wood

N

Stalisfield Road

Rice Wood

4. Turn left along the roadside, pass a junction, again heading for Ospringe, pass an orchard on the left, then another road junction, then go uphill to a third road junction, soon reaching the former oast house noted on the outward route, which is retraced from here to Brogdale Farm.

24. Chilham

A lovely circuit based on a showpiece village, crossing farming countryside, woodland and downland, mainly on very good paths and tracks, with a small amount of minor road. Prolonged ascent from East Stour Farm, at 25 metres (82 ft.) above sea level, to the top of the down at 126m. (414 ft.) above sea level and also a lesser ascent back into the village. No steep gradients, but a slightly rough path for some distance after East Stour Farm. Six stiles.

Distance: 9km (5½ miles).

Start/car parking: Free car park, with public conveniences, beside the main A252 road at the signposted entrance from that road to the village, grid reference 067536.

Maps: Ordnance Survey Explorer 137, Ashford, 1:25,000. Ordnance Survey Landranger 179, Canterbury and East Kent, 1:50,000 or Ordnance Survey Landranger 189, Ashford and Romney Marsh, 1:50,000.

Tea Shop

Picture postcard village, picture postcard tea shop, and the name 'The Copper Kettle' really says all that is needed about this venue. But to enlarge a little, this café has tables outside for sunny days, with the black grapes of the vine hanging overhead. Indoors, the tearooms are cool or cosy depending on the weather and the time of year. Samples from the menu include coffee and biscuits, Kentish cream tea, scones and cakes, savoury dishes including quiche, paté with French bread, and smoked trout with salad. Cooked meals such as sausages with chips, fish and chips, and omelettes are available only until 2.30pm.

Open: Seven days a week, 10am to 5pm, but closed on Mondays from November to April. Tel. 01227 730303.

Introduction

Set well up the side of the downland which presses close around, Chilham is one of Kent's great villages, centred on a small but famous Square, often used for filming, Timber framed buildings blend harmoniously with the 15th-century church and the entrance to the Jacobean mansion, Chilham Castle, an Inigo Jones designed building set in large and beautiful grounds, reworked by Capability Brown in the 18th century. There is also a Norman keep on Roman foundations. The lanes leading to and from the Square also have many fine timbered houses. Two inns, a tea shop and a few varied shops add to the attraction for visitors. The parish church of St. Mary, behind the White Horse Inn, is rich in internal monuments.

The Copper Kettle in Chilham

Nearby

The great historic city of Canterbury, with its marvellous history and its manifold attractions for visitors, is just a few miles along the A252/A28.

Julieberrie Downs long barrow is situated very close to the line of this walk, about 1km (two-thirds of a mile) short of Chilham.

The Walk

Walk uphill along the road leading into the Square. Bear right, past the gates of Chilham Castle, and on down School Hill, passing St. Mary's Primary School. At the bottom, bear right, along Mountain Street, a pleasant traffic-free surfaced lane.

1. In about 750 metres turn left after passing two houses, Monckton Manor being the second. There is a waymark and also a concrete public footpath sign. Follow a little path under trees, leading to a cultivated field. Cross diagonally to the right, heading for the far corner; the signposted exit stile is 30 metres to the left of the corner. After the stile, turn right, to continue over grass, close to a fence on the right. Go over another stile and carry on along the edge of the next meadow, soon reaching a signpost. Bear left from this point, as indicated, towards a gate in the far corner, turning left to cross the River Great Stour on a footbridge. Join the A28, turning left for 70 metres. Cross over and turn right, up a surfaced drive leading to East Stour Farm. Go through a little gate and continue on a broad track, heading for the railway line. Go through a field gate and pass under the railway. Ignore a waymarked stile on the left; go straight on along an agricultural track. In 100 metres or so, fork left to rise on a narrow path under trees, largely beech. Ignore a waymarked stile on the left and continue, the path being rough and a little overgrown in places. Join the route of the waymarked Stour Valley Walk, going straight ahead, still under trees.

2. At a waymarked cross paths, go straight ahead, uphill, the path now more worn. A stile at the top of the wood is by-passed as agricultural downland is reached. Join a more important track in 40 metres, bearing left. Turn left at a waymark on a substantial post, to head towards woodland.

3. In 150 metres, at a post with bridleway and footpath waymarks, keep left, along the bridleway, a good grass track with a cultivated field on the left. Go through a small gate and head into woodland. The track is wide and clear, soon beginning to descend through mixed woodland, including conifers and plenty of beech. Stay with this major track for almost 1.3km

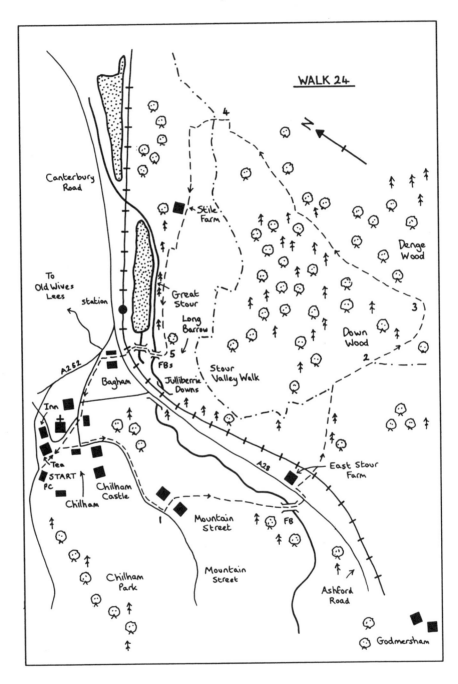

WALK 24

(three-quarters of a mile), ignoring any side tracks, to emerge from the wood and continue across pasture land.

4. Reach a surfaced access roadway, turning left, downhill. Bear to the left at the bottom of the hill and carry on for 150 metres, until the road bends to the right. Go over a stile on the left and take the path worn across a cultivated field, passing a waymark on a post and continuing along the bottom edge of the field to a waymarked stile. Cross a meadow – there is no distinct path on the ground – keeping close to a bank on the left to reach a waymarked stile. Cross the end of a house garden and go over another waymarked stile to join an access roadway. Turn right for 20 metres and then turn left over a stile, to walk along the bottom edge of fields, with Stile Farm on the right. Follow the grass path, angling to the right to stay close to the edge of a belt of trees.

5. Ten metres after leaving the field, turn right at a waymarked post to follow a little path through the trees to the River Stour, with a great willow in front and a large, attractive, former mill to the right. Bear right, along an access drive, to a bridge over the river. The drive is surfaced as it bends to the left to cross another waterway on a bridge, pass a car park for the Chilham Nature Walk and go over the railway on a level crossing. Go straight across the A28 and walk by the side of a minor road towards the A252. Do not join that road, but bear left along roadside pavement to rise steadily on a minor road (The Street) leading directly to the village Square, passing the Woolpack Inn on the way. The tea shop is at the far end of the Square. From the tea shop, retrace the outward route back to the car park.

25. Charing

A pleasing short circular walk, based on a fine village, using minor lanes, part of the ancient Pilgrims' Way and footpaths. One modest ascent but no difficulties underfoot. Four stiles.

Distance: 5km (3 miles).

Start/car parking: Official free car park in front of the church, grid reference 954494.

Maps: Ordnance Survey Explorer 137, Ashford, 1:25,000. Ordnance Survey Landranger 189, Ashford and Romney Marsh, 1:50,000.

Tea Shop

The Pilgrim's Table is a superb historic building on the High Street of this picturesque village. A good range of food and drink is offered with a choice of teas and coffees, soft drinks and fruit juices. Delicious cakes served include carrot cake and coffee gateaux; or for a change try pain au chocolate or a croissant with tea or coffee – Kent is not many miles from France! Soup, sandwiches, and cooked meals are served at lunchtime.

Open: Wednesday to Saturday 10am to 5pm also open on Monday and Tuesday in the summer months. Tel. 01233 712170.

Introduction

A large and attractive village at the foot of the North Downs, Charing is on the contour at which springs emerge as water reaches the impermeable clay below the chalk and is then forced to the surface. Established in medieval times, Charing has a rich history. The Archbishop's Palace was built by Cranmer, Archbishop of Canterbury. Kings Henry VII and VIII were entertained here, the latter liking the palace so well that, diplomatically, Cranmer gave it to him in 1545. Even as long ago as the iron age, the area was crossed by long distance tracks along the top and the bottom of the adjacent Downs. From early medieval times, the Pilgrims' Way linked London with Canterbury, as any reader of Chaucer will know; there was also a Winchester to Canterbury route. Charing was one day's journey away from the destination. Fortunately, the 20th-century routes, such as the A20 and A252 roads and the railway line, by-pass the

Pett Place, Charing

village. Beside the remains of the Palace, the church completes a fine group of old buildings, although the present structure replaces a church burned down in Elizabethan times. The High Street, rising towards the Downs, is lined with elegant buildings, many of them Tudor, now occupied by shops and inns. The railway station has services on the Folkestone, Ashford and London line.

Nearby

The large and important town of Ashford, a rail and road communication centre, is readily accessible from Charing.

The Walk

Walk through the churchyard on the surfaced path which keeps to the right of the church. Continue between the high fences of house gardens, soon reaching an extensive playing field. Bear slightly left across the playing field to pass close to a residential block on the left before reaching a waymarked plank bridge and little gate. Go through the gate and along a well-defined path crossing a cultivated field, rising gently to a stile at the top.. Carry on across meadow grass for a short distance to a stile giving access to the surfaced Pett Lane. Turn right, along the lane, passing the entrance to the stately Pett Place.

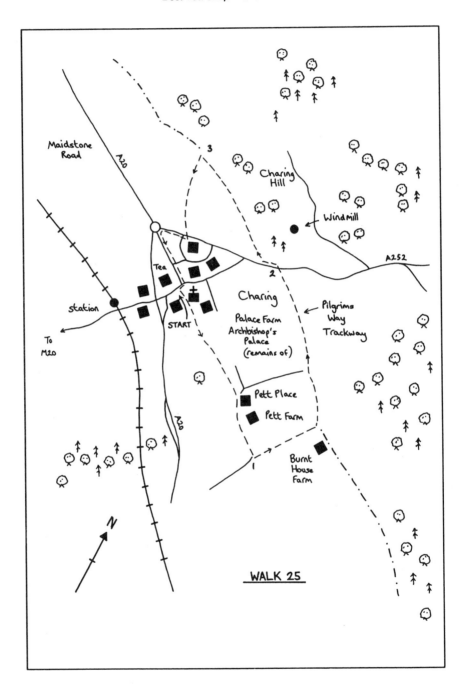

Maidstone Road

A20

Charing Hill

Windmill

A252

Charing

Tea

Palace Farm
Archbishop's
Palace
(remains of)

Pilgrims Way Trackway

station

To M20

START

2

3

Pett Place

Pett Farm

Burnt House Farm

A20

N

WALK 25

1. As the lane bends to the right, turn left at a 'byway' signpost to rise steadily up an apparently old sunken lane between outgrown hedges for 500 metres. At the top turn left at the 'Y' fork by a large beech tree, to follow a minor road. This is part of the ancient Pilgrims' Way and also the modern North Downs Way. Go straight on at a road junction, with another beech tree on an 'island'. Continue, a little up and down, with a windmill visible ahead, to join the A252 road.

2. Turn left along the roadside pavement for 30 metres, then cross and take a well-signposted unsurfaced byway, initially passing a few buildings. Go straight on at a waymarked junction and stay with this fine broad track for almost 1km (two-thirds of a mile), passing a covered reservoir and being reassured by the occasional red waymark.

3. Go over a stile on the left and bear left to follow a defined path across a meadow, heading for Charing village. Pass through two field gates and continue on the same line. Go over a stile to join the A252 road, cross over, then turn right to walk along the wide grass verge towards a roundabout. Before the roundabout, bear left under trees to pass the village fire station and walk up a quiet residential road towards the village centre. On reaching High Street, turn right; the tea shop is a little way down on the right. After refreshment, turn left, back up the High Street, to the right turn which leads to the church and the car park.

26. Leeds Castle

A short, very easy, walk largely through the parkland of Leeds Castle, with the interest of the castle, its lakes and the peripheral buildings. On excellent footpaths, the route also traverses just a little agricultural land and woodland. Rise and fall is slight. Three stiles.

Distance: 3.3km (2 miles).

Start/car parking: A roadside layby for six or seven cars is situated immediately to the north of Broomfield hamlet, which is situated to the south of the A20 main road, grid reference 840527.

Maps: Ordnance Survey Explorer 137, Ashford, 1:25,000 or Ordnance Survey Explorer 148, Maidstone, 1:25,000. Ordnance Survey Landranger 188, Maidstone and the Weald, 1:50,000.

Tea Shop

There are several catering outlets at Leeds Castle ranging from ice cream and fast food stalls in the courtyard to indoor and verandah restaurants. The suggested venue is the Wykeham Martin tearoom, which is part of the Fairfax Hall complex. Counter service here gives an excellent selection of cakes such as apple and cider cake, fudge brownies, carrot cake, and scones served with jam and cream. Just about everything to drink from Coca-Cola to coffee. Lemon was willingly substituted for milk when ordering tea. Hot meals are served between 12 and 3pm.

Open: 10am – 5pm but closes at 3pm in the winter months. Tel. 01622 765400.

Introduction

One of the best known and most historic castle sites in Britain, Leeds had its first structure in late Saxon times, superseded by an early Norman Castle which was rebuilt by King Edward I into the great structure which is largely what we see today, although the defensive castle has, inevitably, been softened into a great palace and there was a good deal of restoration in the 19th century. It has done duty as a fortress, a royal residence (including King Henry VIII) and, until comparatively recently, a private residence. The last private owner, Lady Olive Bailey established the Leeds Castle Foundation as a

Leeds Castle

private charitable trust; the Trust took over responsibility for the castle on her death in 1974. The situation, on two islands surrounded by a lake, is superb and the surrounding gardens and grounds are both extensive (500 acres) and attractive. Inside the castle many rooms, enriched by fine furniture, paintings and tapestries, are open to the public, whilst in the gardens and grounds are ornamental ponds, cascades, vineyard, aviary, maze, grotto, museum of dog collars and golf course. The peripheral buildings include a catering complex based on a 17th-century tithe barn and several themed gift shops.

Nearby

Maidstone (see walk 27).

The Walk

Start by walking south along the minor road, crossing the River Len and continuing uphill through Broomfield hamlet. Pass Church Farm House, dated 1400, and look carefully for a 'public footpath' sign embedded in the hedge on the left.

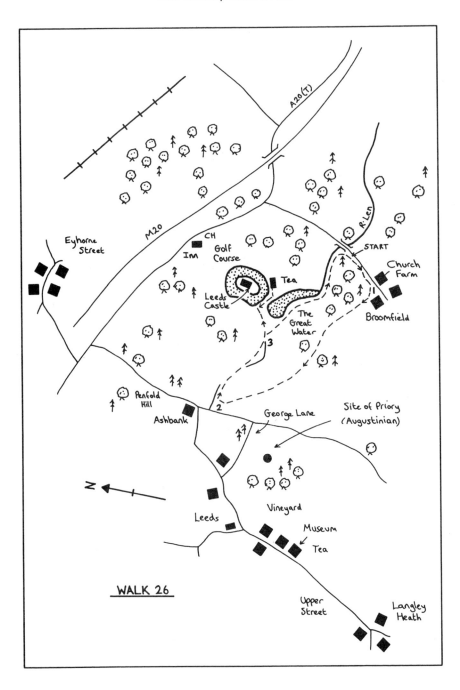

A20(T)

M20

Eyhorne
Street

CH
Im
Golf
Course

R.Len

START

Church
Farm

Tea

Leeds
Castle

Broomfield

The
Great
Water

3

Penfold
Hill
Ashbank

2

George Lane

Site of Priory
(Augustinian)

N

Leeds

Vineyard

Museum
Tea

WALK 26

Upper
Street

Langley
Heath

1. Turn right here, beside Pink Cottage, to rise along a concrete path, which soon becomes a good wide track between hedges. Turn right at a yellow waymark on a post to follow a well-used path with woodland on the right and a large cultivated field on the left, with a first glimpse of the lake and the castle. Pass through light woodland, rising more steeply. Leave the wood at a waymarked gate to continue on a clear path across the bottom end of a huge cultivated field with a fence on the right.

2. Go over a waymarked stile and walk across grass to join a surfaced drive descending towards the castle, now very much in view. Turn right to go down the drive. At a waymarked post go straight ahead over short grass towards a double field gate. Bear right, before the gates, to go up to a small waymarked gate, then turning left to follow the broad roadway heading for the castle. Great Water is to the right and the ruins of the former barbican and water mill are to the left. Bear right to cross the broad causeway between lakes, then turn right to rise to the complex which includes the tea shop and other refreshment opportunities, around a courtyard. After refreshment return across the causeway, then bear left to a wooden 'bus stop' shelter.

3. Turn left opposite the shelter, over grass, to reach a waymarked stile on the Len Way in 60 metres. Follow a distinct path, uphill over rough grass initially, with the occasional waymark. Keep close to Great Water, well-provided with waterfowl, including black swans. Go over a waymarked stile and into woodland, cross a footbridge over the River Len and continue along an excellent grass path between the trees, reaching the minor public road at the car parking layby.

27. Aylesford

Not a country walk, but a stroll through an attractive historic village, combined with a visit to The Friars, a remarkable blend of religious centre and visitor attraction. The walking is entirely on hard surfaces, with no necessity for boots. No stiles or other impediments.

Distance: 2km (1⅓ miles).

Start/car parking: Free public car park at the main entrance to the village, sandwiched between the High Street and the River Medway, grid reference 731589.

Maps: Ordnance Survey Explorer 148, Maidstone, 1:25,000. Ordnance Survey Landranger 188, Maidstone and the Weald, 1:50,000.

Tea Shop

The Friars provides a peaceful and reflective environment. The cafeteria here is housed in a completely renovated, large thatched barn – note the superb timber work and substantial beams. The catering style is somewhat

The tea shop at Aylesford

basic and drinks are served in plastic cups; nevertheless the venue is quite adequate for morning coffee, light lunch, or afternoon tea; prices are reasonable.

Open: Monday to Saturday, 10am to 5pm and Sunday 11am to 5pm. Closes at 4pm in the winter months. Tel 01622 717272.

Introduction

Squeezed between the extensive suburbs of Maidstone, the M20 and large paper mills, Aylesford remains a relatively unspoilt village in a rather uncomfortable environment. The village is allegedly on the site of a great battle, fought in AD55 between the long established British and the invading Jutes, led by Hengist and Horsa. The latter won, with the consequential founding of the English nation by a mixture of Angles, Saxons and Jutes. Subsequently great battles were fought over the same territory in the 9th and 10th centuries.

The historic buildings in Aylesford include the Chequers, smallest inn in Kent, Sedley Almshouses of 1605 and the church of St. Peter and St. Paul, standing above the village. The church is basically 15th century, with a Norman tower, spacious and with much to see inside, including a nicely decorated organ and an (over?) ornate carved memorial in one corner. Medway Bridge is of 14th-century origin; two central arches being replaced by one longer span in 1824 to allow larger vessels to sail up the Medway.

The village street has shops, inns and restaurants.

The Friars was founded in 1242 as a priory when the first Carmelites arrived from the Holy Land. Dissolved by King Henry VIII in 1537, it became a private dwelling for more than four centuries until, in 1949, the Carmelites regained possession of their old home. Today the complex is a popular pilgrimage centre, with guesthouse and conference facilities. The extensive buildings are a rich blend of medieval and modern, with several chapels containing outstanding works of modern religious art. The spacious site also includes craft workshops and a medieval barn converted into shop and café. Public access to the site is encouraged; opening hours are from dawn to dusk each day.

Nearby

The county town of Maidstone is very close. The town centre still has some historic buildings such as the Archbishops' Palace by the side of the River Medway, but the overall ambience is of a busy, prosperous, shopping centre. The Museum of Kent Life is at nearby Cobtree on the northern fringe of the town.

The much damaged remains of Kits Coty neolithic long barrow

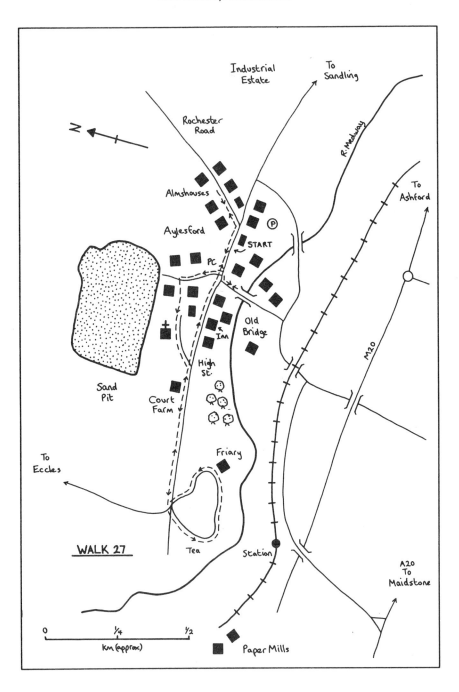

N

To
Sandling

Industrial
Estate

Rochester
Road

R. Medway

To
Ashford

Almshouses

Aylesford

START

PC

P

Sand
Pit

Old
Bridge

Inn

M20

High
St.

Court
Farm

To
Eccles

Friary

A20
To
Maidstone

Tea

Station

WALK 27

0   ¼   ½

km (approx)

Paper Mills

and of Lower Kits Coty burial chamber are approximately two kilometres (1⅓ miles) north east of Aylesford.

The Walk

Leave the car park by a track signposted 'High Street'. Go through a gate and cross an ornamental garden behind a restaurant. Go through another gate to join the High Street. Proceed along Rochester Road for about 50 metres to see the Sedley Almshouses, set on a grass bank to the left.

Return to the junction, turning right to pass the public conveniences, then go to the right, up Church Walk. Fork left to continue to the church, well worth a visit if open. Carry on along a footpath to rejoin the main street and go on past the entrance to Court Farm, along the roadside as far as the Friars.

Turn left at the bend in the road to reach the entrance to the complex, a most interesting place even for totally non-religious visitors for, at the very least, a stroll through the gardens and appreciation of the old and not so old buildings.

Return to the village along the roadside footpath, staying with the High Street as it dips, then admiring the wonderful array of historic buildings. As a very short diversion, it is worth making a right turn in the village centre, where a now minor road crosses the Medway on the old bridge. Return to the High Street to retrace the outward route to the car park. *Alternatively, there is a riverside path straight back to the car park; its use would mean missing out some nice old buildings in the High Street.*

28. Knole and Ightham Mote

A splendid circular walk through attractive countryside, linking two of the National Trust's finest Kent properties, using a length of the Greensand Way and other good tracks, including those through Knole Park and a route organised by the National Trust. Close to the mid point of the circuit is One Tree Hill, another National Trust land holding with a free car park. This car park can be used as a focal point to divide the walk into two shorter walks, each with its own tea shop. Some rise and fall, climbing One Tree Hill from each direction, but not excessive and at reasonable gradients. Some mud is possible; six stiles.

Distance: 12km (7½ miles). Shorter walks – One Tree Hill to Knole and back, 5km (3½ miles). One Tree Hill to Ightham Mote and back, 6.5km (4 miles).

Start/car parking: Spacious free car park at Ightham Mote, open all year, grid reference 584535. For shorter walks, free car park at One Tree Hill, grid reference 559532.

Maps: Ordnance Survey Explorer 147, Sevenoaks and Tonbridge, 1:25,000. Ordnance Survey Landranger 188, Maidstone and the Weald, 1:50,000.

Tea Shop

The Brew House at Knole Park provides a suitable venue for refreshment part way round this walk and can be accessed even if not visiting the stately home. Cream teas are served; there is a superb choice of cakes including old-fashioned, cream-filled Victoria sponge, and ginger cake with lemon topping. Good coffee – choice of tea including the National Trust own blend; cold drinks include really good lemonade. Cooked meals are available at lunch time with ploughman's or hop picker's lunches providing a slightly lighter option. Outside is a very sheltered courtyard with benches and seats for those preferring to stay in the open air.

Open: Beginning of April (or Easter if earlier) to end of October – Wednesday To Saturday 11am to 4.30pm. Also open Sunday Good Friday and Bank Holiday Mons. and November and December

Ightham Mote

Except on Monday & Tuesday. If in any doubt confirm by telephone. Tel 01732 743748.

Should you wish to have refreshment before or at the end of the walk the tea pavilion at Ightham Mote offers an attractive combination of indoor and outdoor catering. Snacks offered include soup, sandwiches and ploughman's lunches; coffee, tea, cold drinks, ice cream and an array of cakes and pastries are always available at the counter. Note – unlike the tea room, the toilets here are beyond the ticket office and can be accessed only by National Trust members or those paying for admission to the property.

Open: Early April to end of October 11am to 5pm but closed on Tuesday and Saturday. Hours in October and May vary depending on the weather. Tel.01732 811314.

Introduction

Sitting well-concealed in a beautiful valley, Ightham Mote is without doubt one of the finest moated medieval manor houses in the country. Originally of the 14th century it has been extensively remodelled through the centuries without impairing its attraction as a medieval building. Inside, the great hall is still magnificent and there are many other striking features. Ightham Mote is surrounded by extensive grounds and well-stocked gardens. Colour coded trails have been organised in the surrounding countryside. The house and gardens are open to the public on most days during the normal National Trust season.

Knole Park, situated on the fringe of Sevenoaks, is very different, a huge stately pile standing prominent in its vast area of park land, which easily accommodates a golf course. 'One of the great Treasure Houses of England', Knole has 365 rooms, 52 staircases, 7 court-yards, and a staggering array of priceless furniture and paintings. Thomas Bourchier, Archbishop of Canterbury, bought Knole in 1456, transforming it from a modest medieval manor house to a great palace. A century later it came into the possession of King Henry VIII, who enlarged it even further. Later given to Thomas Sackville by Queen Elizabeth I, it was held by that family for many genera-tions. The house is open to the public on some days each week during the normal National Trust season. The gardens are open on only one day each month from May to September. The great park, with its herds of fallow and Sika deer, is open throughout the year by courtesy of Lord Sackville.

One Tree Hill is an attractive area of natural woodland in the care of the National Trust, criss-crossed by many trails.

Nearby

The attractive country town of Sevenoaks has a good High Street, a museum and a theatre and is a comprehensive shopping centre.

The Walk

From Ightham Mote car park, walk down past the ticket office towards the tea pavilion, bearing left then right to pass through the staff car park and reach a lane at the bottom. Turn right to pass along the side of the house, then bear left through ornamental gates to join the public road. Turn right, along the roadside, for 40 metres.

1. Turn left along a 'bridle path' at the far end of Mote Farm. You are now on the Greensand Way, all the way to Knole. Bear right, uphill, at a junction with a four oast building on the left, in 100 metres to continue the ascent on a broad, stony, track. Go straight ahead at a fork, passing a little wood on the left. Carry on under trees at an open gate. The way is easy to follow here; one section has very long views to the south. Pass Wilmot Cottage and continue, now on an earth surface. Turn right, up steps, by a waymarked post, then turn left to resume the line at the bottom edge of woodland; there is plenty of bramble along the way. Reach a waymarked stile and leave the National Trust property along a tightly fenced section of the path to another waymarked stile, soon joining a very minor surfaced road.

2. Turn right to follow the sign, steeply uphill. As the road ends by a house entrance, turn left, up steps, at a 'Greensand Way' sign, then ascend through woodland on a good path. Go over a stile and enter the National Trust 'One Tree Hill' land. Pass a seat at a junction and go straight on, keeping to the Greensand Way, ignoring the many other tracks in this open access area. *(Those who have opted for the shorter Ightham Mote only walk can bear right for the most direct route back to the One Tree Hill car park).* Pass a concrete seat and go slightly downhill; there are waymarks from time to time. Leave the National Trust land under a barrier to reach a minor road. *(Last opportunity to turn right to return to the One Tree Hill car park).*

3. Turn left downhill, then fork right in a few metres at a footpath

sign by Shepherd's Mead. Fork right again before the house gate, to carry on between fences, with many beech trees to the right. Go over a stile and bear right. In 20 metres bear left to a waymarked stile and a locked gate. Go diagonally across a paddock, the way marked by posts. At the far side, turn slightly left to find a waymarked stile and a path through some woodland, reaching a minor road.

4. Go across the road and enter the Knole Estate through a tall, narrow, gate. Follow a well-worn track, cross the wide, semi-surfaced Chestnut Walk and go straight on along a lesser roadway, through an area covered in bracken. Reach Broad Walk, going across to a path between bracken, with plenty of deer evident. Continue along a track which, initially, heads for the corner of the garden wall, then bears left to stay parallel with the wall between a wide-spaced avenue of oaks. Pass ornamental metal gates then, at the corner of the property, turn right at a waymark to walk across the front of the house, passing the public entrance. *(Bear left, away from the house, to walk on to Sevenoaks town, less than 1km (½ mile) further, along an obvious path or using the exit roadway. A tea shop is found by turning right for 100 metres at the point where the Knole driveway joins a main street.)* The Knole tearoom is found by following the 'tea room and toilets' sign close to the far end of the house frontage. To return, turn right on leaving the tearoom and follow the garden wall, uphill, for a short distance. At the start of an avenue of trees bear left along a grass track, heading towards a golf course. Join a surfaced roadway and stay with it as it weaves to and from through the course. Eventually, pass a pond on the right, then Keeper's Cottage, then the end of the Chestnut Walk, before joining the public road through a tall, narrow, gate.

5. Go across to follow a minor road towards Underriver and Hildenborough, passing a pond with lilies on the left. Pass Weald Height Farm entrance on the right, going downhill to a junction.

6. Go straight across to continue the circuit on a signposted bridleway. *(Turn right for 60 metres to return to the One Tree Hill*

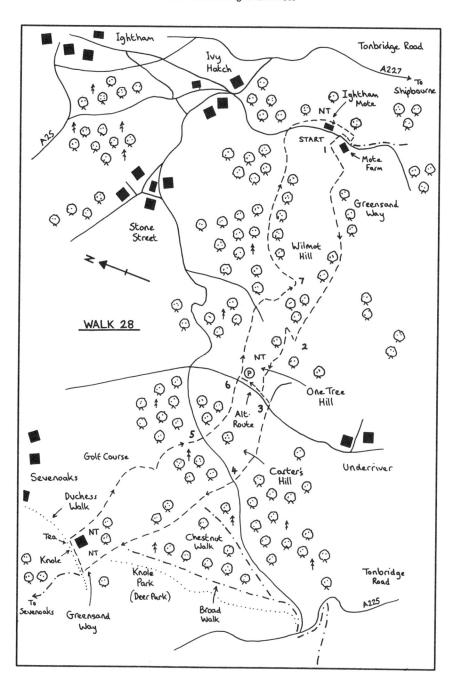

car park to finish the Knole shorter walk). The bridleway keeps close to the National Trust boundary fence for some distance, basically a good track but with some horse-churned mud. Pass a seat and bear to the right at the next junction, still close to the National Trust fence. Descend, then rise again. Keep right at a fork, then go left, on the wider track, at the next fork, soon reaching a surfaced access drive. Go straight across to continue along 'public bridleway', with an apple orchard on the right. At a junction, ignore the blue waymark, going straight ahead through a waymarked opening along a narrow footpath.

7. At a junction turn left, under a horse barrier, and follow the National Trust green-waymarked Ightham walk. Pass a seat, descend past a barrier, and carry on along a good little path. Go straight across a broader track, then pass a barrier, still on the green route, in a shallow valley, with lush vegetation including a great deal of bay willow herb. Go through a wood, gently downhill. Pass a pond on the right, then a barrier, join a more major track and bear right. Reach the public road and go straight across to pass a gate and a muddy area before going uphill under trees, up steps and bearing to the right, into the Ightham Mote entrance drive, just before the car park.

Also of Interest:

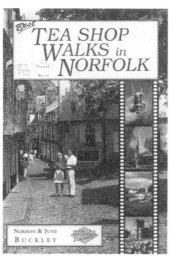

BEST TEA SHOP WALKS IN NORFOLK

Norman & June Buckley

25 gentle walks, suitable for all the family, spread throughout Norfolk's countryside and coastline. Most routes are centred on Norfolk's towns, villages and stately homes, and all feature essential information on the landscape, social and industrial history, and interesting features met along the way. Norman & June Buckley, Britain's tea shop walk experts, believe that a 'tea shop stop' adds a whole new dimension to country walking, and this new title contains a huge range of establishments - some in out of the way and unusual places. £6.95

BEST TEA SHOP WALKS IN SURREY & SUSSEX

Margaret & Barrie Howard

A leisurely walk in the long-neglected countryside of Surrey and Sussex followed by a delicious afternoon tea. "An enjoyable mixture of rambling and relaxation...This book offers a quintessentially English slice of life." SURREY ADVERTISER £6.95

BEST TEA SHOP WALKS IN SUFFOLK

Michael Anderton

Walk through Suffolk's wide diversity of terrain - from the coastal margin of the Heritage Coast to the valleys of the river Stour, Deben and Gipping - and sample the best of the county's 3500 miles of public path. And after your walk, why not reward yourself with a few home made cakes at one of the unusual tea shops featured on the routes? £6.95

... Plus many more of the very best Tea Shop Walks throughout England and Wales. Check our web site or catalogue!

HOLIDAY WALKS IN THE DORDOGNE

Norman Buckley

Descriptions of more than 25 walks spread over this prime holiday area are included in a style which will appeal to the British holiday visitor and English-speaking resident alike. The routes are set out in a logical manner and are accompanied by interesting features to see along the way. Beautiful river valleys, plentiful woodland, ancient towns, villages and castles plus local visitor attractions and refreshment possibilities entice the most reluctant walker to explore and fully appreciate this truly magnificent area. Easy-to-follow maps are also included, essential for visitors to any area but particularly important when travelling abroad, and a selection of both colour and black and white photographs complete this excellent package. £8.95

NORTH WALES WALKING ON THE LEVEL

Norman Buckley

25 circular walks in the hills and mountains of North Wales, intended for those who enjoy gentle walking in fine surroundings but do not wish to make significant ascents. Route maps, descriptions of towns and villages, landscape and interesting features are all included. There is a summary of each walk, including length and total ascent. £6.95

LAKELAND WALKING ON THE LEVEL

Norman Buckley

Walk among the highest mountains of Lakeland and avoid the steep ascents - with no compromises on the views! "A good spread of walks" RAMBLING TODAY. £6.95